Jack Garbutt

The Bilsdale Bombardier

Jack Garbutt

The Bilsdale Bombardier

Susan N Laffey

Waltersgill

Published in 2008 by:
Waltersgill
Photography & Publishing,
17 Wrenbeck Drive, Otley,
West Yorkshire, LS21 2BP.

ISBN 978 0 9556454 1 9

Designed By:
Waltersgill.

Printed and bound by:
Smith Settle
Gateway Drive, Yeadon,
West Yorkshire, LS19 7XY.

Acknowledgements

I would like to thank the following people who have encouraged and helped me turn my research on Jack Garbutt, my great-uncle, into this book:

Gladys Wilmore - for sparking my interest in the first place.

Ken and Judy Garbutt - for fanning the flames during holiday trips around Europe.

Agnes Leckenby and Arthur Frankland - for tales of Bilsdale and Wingroves.

The Garbutt cousins - Leslie Garbutt, Cliff Garbutt, Val Holtby, John Garbutt, Beryl Wood, Eileen Brindle, Molly Scott, Ruth Rudd, Michael Garbutt, Sharon Williams, Barrie Welbourn and Anne Atkinson - for helping make sure the facts about Jack's siblings were correct.

Phil Ginnings - for keeping me straight on the history.

Ida Atkinson - for her wealth of information and research on all things Bilsdale and for persuading me to do a talk for the Bilsdale Study Group which meant this book got written.

Daniel Walters of Waltersgill Publications - for calmly and professionally turning my manuscript into a book.

Janet Winterbottom - for proof reading and constant encouragement.

Tom Laffey - for IT support, infinite patience and understanding.

For Uncle Jack and the Garbutts from Bilsdale,
past, present and future.

If I should die, think only this of me:
That there's some corner of a foreign field
That is forever England.

From The Soldier by Rupert Brooke.[1]

Contents

Map of Northern France and Belguim 1914- 1919   8

Introduction   9

Chapter 1.   The Garbutts of Bilsdale   11

Chapter 2.   Life at Wingroves in 1900   26

Chapter 3.   School Years   33

Chapter 4.   1914-1915 - The Great Adventure   49

            Letters 1914-15   65

            War Diary 1915   74

Chapter 5.   1916 - The Somme   87

            Letters 1916   98

            War Diary 1916   109

Chapter 6.   1917 - Passchendaele   134

            Letters 1917   150

            War Diary 1917   168

Chapter 7.   1918 - The Spring Offensive   188

            Letters 1918   196

            War Diary 1918   197

Chapter 8.   Afterwards   204

            War Diary 1918-1919   216

Appendix 1 Soldiers from Bilsdale   238

References   244

Notes and Abbreviations   250

Bibliography   253

Authors Note   259

Northern France and Belguim 1914 - 1919

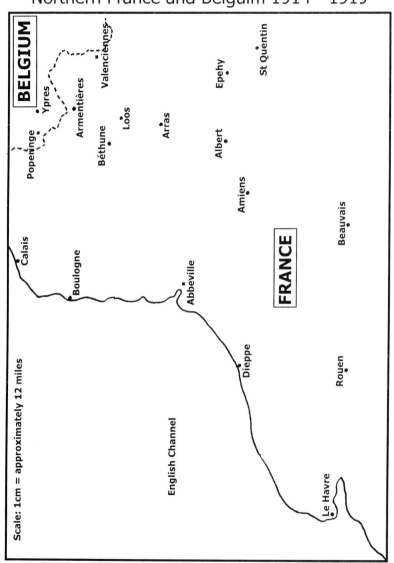

Introduction

This is the story of John William (Jack) Garbutt. He was an ordinary man who was born at a remote farm in Bilsdale near Stokesley in North Yorkshire and spent the first 18 years of his life in that county or in County Durham. He did not have any educational opportunities and was a farm labourer for most of his teenage years, although he later became a policeman. If the First World War had not happened, he would probably never have travelled far from home but instead he enlisted in the Royal Field Artillery in the Autumn of 1914 and spent the next three and a half years in France and Belgium. He started as a Gunner but was promoted in 1917 and for that reason I have nick-named him the Bilsdale Bombardier.

In 1914, life in Bilsdale, and communities like it, had hardly changed for centuries and was certainly not some kind of rural idyll for the subsistence farmers and their families who worked the land. However, life for Jack and millions of similar men from all over Europe was changed forever by the Great War. To understand the true significance and impact of the War, we need to understand the historical background of Jack's world and his family who had always lived in Bilsdale. Through an examination of his forebears we can gain an insight into what type of world he lived in and understand the contrast between this and what he was to experience as a soldier. We can reflect on how his upbringing may have influenced his way of coping with the conditions of war, perhaps even his reasons for signing up. It can certainly give us insight into how going to war must have seemed like a big adventure and an opportunity to experience life away from rural hardship. Like most of his friends, Jack probably shared the belief that it would be all over by Christmas; he would certainly have had no awareness of what war was going to be like.

Jack's story is a reflection of what was happening all over the nation; young men were removed from their own locality to locations, environments and conditions never before imagined and still barely believable. That any of these men survived can be surprising; that so many died is shocking. As the 90th anniversary of the Armistice approaches it is fitting that Jack's story is preserved in this book. He is not famous, nor is he distinguished, but he is a symbol of all the ordinary men from Bilsdale and around the world who did their bit when the call came.

Chapter 1
The Garbutts of Bilsdale

The name Garbutt comes from the teutonic phrase pronounced Ger bodo and meaning Spear Herald[1]. No-one knows when the first "spear herald" appeared in North Yorkshire but as the word "teutonic" refers to peoples from the north of Germany, Denmark and southern Norway and Sweden, I have always believed that the first Garbutts arrived during the Viking invasions which took place from around 787-1066AD.

What we can be certain of is the fact that there have been Garbutts in Bilsdale as far back as records go. For example in the Rievaulx Cartulary records from 1540 the name in a variety of spellings - Garbote, Garbotte and Garbutt - is seen among the records of tenants.[2]

There are several branches of the Garbutt family in the Dale - surely a fantastic research opportunity for a DNA expert would be to see if there is a common link between the families - but this book is about a branch of the family that has been traced back as far as the 1770s.

Robert (Senior)

In the Bilsdale *Rental for Audit at Lady Day*[3] records of 1772 the tenants of Clay House Farm (originally known as Jop Yate [Chop Gate] Farm) are recorded as a Mary Garbutt and Hannah Hoggard. The rent for the farm was £2 11s 3d to be paid twice per year at Michaelmas (29th September) and Lady Day (25th March). In 1780-81 Mary is listed as being the tenant with her son Robert and with Hannah, and from 1782 to 1785 Mary and Robert were the sole tenants. A Hannah Hoggard living at William Beck was buried in 1787; perhaps this was the same person who had gone to live with different relatives.

There is no mention of a husband for Mary and no records exist for tenants of Clay House from 1743-1772. Sadly, at the moment we have no way of knowing the name of Robert's father.

Robert was the sole tenant of Clay House Farm from 1786 to 1802. The rent was £5 0s 0d in 1786, rising to £6 5s 0d in 1799.

On 28th February 1782 Robert married Hannah Garbutt. They had four children: Pally born in about 1782, John in 1783, Robert in 1786 and Thomas in 1789.

Robert (Junior)

Robert senior died in 1800 and was buried on 6th December. His son Robert junior took over the tenancy of Clay House Farm with his mother Hannah and in 1802 their rent was £7 2s 6d.

Robert married Hannah Trousdale, daughter of Thomas Trousdale from what is now known as Dale View Farm, originally Seave Green, Farm on 5th January 1815. Robert and Hannah had eight children:

1. Robert, baptised on 14th August 1815.
2. John, baptised on 22nd December 1816. He was blind (possibly following a cold) by the age of 29 and was musical - he led the singing at the Primitive Methodist Chapel before they got an organ.[4] He lived with his brother Stephen at Clay House and died in 1894.
3. William, baptised on 18th March 1821. He married Jane Ainsley and was a husbandman (a farmer, often one who worked with animals) at the time of his marriage, although I believe he also worked as a stonemason. He lived at Laddle Gill and died on 30th January 1885.
4. Joseph, baptised on 27th December 1823.
5. Stephen, baptised on 28th August 1825. He married Jane Bell in 1856 and lived at Clay House. He died in 1890.

6.   Isaac, baptised on 26th August 1827.
7.   Philip, baptised on 23rd May 1830 and buried on 2nd January 1834.
8.   George, baptised on 3rd June 1832. In June 1855 he married Ann Bentley and they had eight children. At the time of his marriage he was a husbandman and he and his wife lived first at Urra and later, by 1861, at Seave Green Farm, which was originally his uncle's farm. He was a Primitive Methodist Lay Preacher and he may have had the first threshing machine in the Dale. He died on 14th January 1916.

Robert died on 6th May 1865, five years after his wife Hannah.

Isaac (Senior)

Issac (Senior) about 1900

Robert's sixth son, Isaac, was born in 1827. On 7th December 1850 he married Dinah Hugill. She was the daughter of William and Elizabeth of Ellermire and was born in 1823 and at the time of the marriage Isaac was a husbandman. Isaac and Dinah lived at several farms in Bilsdale. In 1851 they lived at Hawterley and in 1858 at The Green. However, by 1861, Isaac and his family had moved to a farm known as Wingroves, and in the 1881 census Isaac is noted as being a farmer of 41+ acres at that property. According to family legend Isaac was the village pig killer and Dinah spent her leisure time in the evenings smoking a long stemmed clay pipe around the open-hearthed turf fire.[5] Dinah died in 1893. Isaac died on 13th May 1906.

Dinah and Isaac had five children:

1. Hannah, baptised on 2nd April 1851. She married a miner, Thomas Wise, in 1873. They had at least eight children.
2. William, baptised on 4th February 1853.
3. George, baptised on 13th July 1856. He married Margaret Hoggart on 22nd January 1881 and they lived at Hagg House from 1884 until at least 1891, and then, by 1898 they lived at Cockflet. They had nine children. George died on 22nd December 1918.
4. Elizabeth, baptised on 11th September 1858. In 1876 she gave birth to a son, Robert, who seems to have been brought up by her parents at Wingroves. He later moved to Nottingham and worked for the Great Northern Railway Police Force. Later, on 27th November 1880, Elizabeth married William Hugill of Beakhills, son of Christopher, and they had seven children. During the mid-1890s the family left Bilsdale and moved to Darlington then Bishop Auckland.
5. Isaac, baptised on 15th February 1861.

Isaac (Junior)

Isaac and Dinah's last child, also called Isaac, was born during a difficult time in the Dale. On the page of St. Hilda's Church baptism register covering 31st January to 23rd May 1861 there are eight baptisms listed. Of these, seven are noted to have been done "privately" - private baptism was typically carried out in the home if it was feared that the child would not survive - and at least four of these, John William Leng, Garbutt Todd,

Elizabeth Peckitt and Jane Anne Wilkinson are noted to have "since died". Isaac himself is noted to be "poorly".[6]

Isaac did survive and on 29th August 1894 he married Mary Emma Hardwick.

Isaac (Junior)   Mary Emma

Mary Emma, who was sometimes known as Molly, was born on 25th December 1874 in Ware Street, Stockton on Tees and was the daughter of Robert Hardwick, a clerk in a shipyard, and Mary, née Heatley. Mary, born in York, was blind and according to family rumour, was an opera singer. I have found no evidence that she sang professionally but from 1859 until at least 1864 a Miss Heatley, a vocalist, was a member of Stockton Amateur Music Society.[7]

During Mary Emma's childhood the family moved from Stockton to Sunderland where we can assume her father found work in a different shipyard. By 1881 however the Hardwicks had returned to Teesside and were living in Hallifield Street, Norton. The family must have been reasonably affluent; by 1881 they also had one servant. Mary Emma had six siblings and seems to have been especially close to Lily who was the youngest.

Sometime after 1891 Mary Emma came to Bilsdale for the air as her health was not good and she became Isaac senior's housekeeper.

Isaac and Mary Emma are well remembered in Bilsdale. In 2002 Agnes Leckenby told me that Isaac was the last person to do the "bidding" (as in "You are bidden [invited] to the funeral of ...") in the Dale. Mary Emma became the village midwife and, when times got hard in the 1920s and 1930s, she worked for a Mrs Peacock cleaning Forge Cottage for one shilling per day.

There are several family stories about Isaac recounted to me by his granddaughter Ruth.

Grandad Garbutt, who was nicknamed ARK, was always a very old man to me. I remember him sitting on a chair by the fire, resting his leg. Some years before he was kicked by a horse and the wound developed into a huge ulcer from which he suffered greatly.

Granny Garbutt used to tell us the tale of Grandad returning from the cattle market late in the evening. On this occasion she had left the washing line hanging across the yard, and Grandad, speeding in on horse and trap, caught his one and only tooth on the line and extracted it. I believe the air was blue!

Our dad, Harry, told us of a Christmas when he was very young. Grandad was busy making frumety, a traditional kind of porridge made from wheat which was eaten on Christmas Eve. Dad was swinging a teddy bear round by its leg when it burst and the sawdust stuffing flew into the pan. According to dad he made a hasty exit to bed and I don't blame him.[8]

In the 1930s Isaac and Mary Emma moved to Northwoods Farm in Bilsdale and their son Harry took over Wingroves Farm. Later still they moved to High Fields Farm, South Broughton.

Isaac died on 4th May 1940 in Great Broughton of cardiac failure, amyloid disease (degenerative ulcer of the veins) and chronic varicose ulceration and he was buried on 7th May 1940 at St. Hilda's Church. When probate was granted on his will in London on 6th August 1940, he left £148 16s 8d to Mary Emma.

Mary Emma lived for nearly 20 more years before dying on 7th July 1959 in Great Broughton, of cachexia (extreme debility) and carcinoma of stomach. She too is buried in St. Hilda's Churchyard although neither her grave, nor Isaac's, is marked.

Isaac and Mary Emma had twelve children between 1895 and 1917.

Bob

The eldest son was Robert Isaac, born on 14th December 1894. Known as Bob, he started work as a policeman in Hartlepool sometime before the First World War and he was present at the German bombardment of the town on 16th December 1914. Bob left the police force although he did later become a special constable. It appears that he also tried to join the army and did some training at Withernsea, but he was apparently told that it was more important that he return home to work on the land. He married Mary Allison and farmed at Midnight Farm, Ingleby Greenhow.

Bob and Mary had three children, Stanley Isaac, Leslie William and John Clifford, but sadly Bob died aged 40 from pneumonia following a bout of the flu. He was buried on 26th February 1935.

The second child, and main character of this book, was John William. He was known as Jack and was born on 10th January 1896. We will hear more about him later.

After Jack, the next child was Edwin, known as Ed, who was baptised on 20th March 1898. He was a farmer at Northwoods Farm and he married Eliza Jane Williams on 26th November 1932. She had come to the Dale to work for Agnes Leckenby's aunt. In the 1940s he moved to Wingroves and later to Stonehouse near Fangdale Beck. He was a Churchwarden of St. John's Church at Fangdale Beck and for the last two years of his life he lived at Dale End, Kirkbymoorside. He died in Scarborough Hospital, and was buried on 3rd March 1964, at St.

Ed

John's Church. Eliza died in a nursing home in Malton in October 1997. Ed and Eliza had one daughter, Beryl, who was born on 8th April 1934.

Next in our story is Gladys Mary, born on 27th January 1900. At the age of about 14 she went to the Vicarage to assist Miss Parry, the sister of the Vicar. She left Bilsdale aged about 16 to study commercial subjects at Nottingham Business College. In Nottingham she lived with her father's cousin Robert and his wife Ada. From the latter stages of the First World War until December 1919 Gladys worked in the Army Pay Corps in Nottingham.

Whilst on holiday in Blackpool with her friend May she met Harry Wilmore, who was from Nelson in Lancashire, and they

Gladys

were married in the Burnley area in 1922. A move to Bradford followed in 1926 and Gladys commenced a long career in a clerical capacity with the Rechabite Friendly Society. This organisation, formed in the mid 19th Century, was strong in West Yorkshire and Lancashire and its members where noted as being teetotal.

Gladys and Harry had one daughter, Eileen, who was born on 27th March 1923 and who still lives in Yorkshire with her family. Harry died in 1963 and Gladys in 1992.

A second daughter for Isaac and Mary Emma was Diana, known as Ana, born in 1902. On 18th February 1922 she married Robert Hartgrove Passman who was a lengthman (someone responsible for looking after a particular stretch of road) in Bilsdale and also a woodman, of Mount Pleasant, Broughton Banks. They lived in Great Broughton and had three children, Hazel, Molly and Jack. Robert died in 1957 and Ana in 1993.

The next child born at Wingroves was Harry on 5th March 1903. Harry

Ana

left school when he was 12 years old and was sent to work on a farm in Ripon where he was paid £4 0s 0d a year. Thereafter he had several jobs before becoming a farmer at Ingleby Hill, at Ingleby Barwick. This was a large farm owned by Mr Ralph

Moore, a widely-known auctioneer as well as a farmer. At Ingleby Hill Harry met Ena Wilson, a miner's daughter from Etherley near Bishop Auckland, who was employed as a domestic servant and cook. They were married on 15th November 1926.

Harry

After their marriage they continued to live at Ingleby Hill before moving back to the Dale to Wingroves in May 1932 after Harry's father had moved to Northwoods Farm.

Times were very hard at Wingroves. In the winter of 1932-33 there was a terrible snowstorm; the snow was so deep that Harry had to dig tunnels to reach the animals and Ena walked 3½ miles over every hedge to get provisions. There was also extreme weather in the summers with very high temperatures in two of the three years the family lived there and as a result the crops failed. This meant staying in the Dale was not financially viable and after three years, in March 1935, the family moved to Rose Cottage, Seamer. After a time they moved to Manor Farm, Carlton-in-Cleveland then to Holme Terrace, Great Broughton before a final move to Healey House Farm, a mile and a half from Sedgefield, in the early days of the Second World War. Harry and Ena lived there until his retirement in the early 1970s when they moved into a bungalow in Sedgefield village.

Sedgefield is about 25 miles from Bilsdale but there are connections between the two areas which explain why Harry and Ena moved to that particular area. Mr Moore, the owner of Ingleby Hill, also owned Sedgefield's Auction Mart and Mr Coward, the landlord of High Fields Farm occupied by Isaac and Mary Emma, also came from the village. Mary Emma used to visit her son and his wife once a year when she came to Sedgefield to pay the rent.

Harry and Ena had six children, Ruth, Doreen, Bobby, who died of meningitis aged one year, Kenneth, Raymond and Alan. Harry and Ena, who were both born on 5th March in different years, both died on 17th July, Ena in 1978 and Harry in 1995.

Isaac and Mary Emma's next child was also son, Stephen, who was born on 22nd November 1904. Stephen had meningitis as a boy and spent much of his life as a patient at Clifton Hospital, York. He died of pneumonia on 9th September 1961.

A sixth son, Arthur Thomas, was born on 18th August 1906. Arthur, known as Tom, married twice and had four children, Wilfred, Kathleen, Paul and Michael. Tom lived on a small holding in Rudby and Cowton near Northallerton before moving to Cloughton near Scarborough in the early 1950s where he managed a farm at The Old Mill for Mr Fox-Lynton, a prominent surgeon. He farmed both arable and livestock and bred heavy horses for farm work and showing. He was featured several times in the Scarborough Mercury in the 1950s, for example feeding the sheep in extreme weather.

Tom

When Mr Fox-Lynton died, Tom left The Old Mill and moved to Wilberfoss near York where he transformed a run down property and became a freelance gardener.

Tom is remembered as a meticulous man, a perfectionist in his work and he enjoyed telling humourous tales. He loved the countryside, especially Bilsdale and enjoyed walking. Sadly, Tom had a stroke on the eve of Michael's wedding day in June 1983 and died two days later. Part of the collection from his funeral purchased a cup that is presented yearly to achievers in the East Yorkshire Riding for the Disabled organisation.

The next child, also a son, George, was born on 28th May 1908. He married Freda Pink and had two children, Howard and Sharon. In his younger days he worked on farms in the Bilsdale area - he collected milk churns for Arthur Sanderson and worked for Mr Frankland at Thornaby in the 1930s. He was given the nickname "Old Whitehead" because of his very fair hair.

After his marriage, the family moved to North Ormsby and George worked for Cochrane's Iron Foundry making castings. He spent his spare time around the house with his children and is remembered as a real family man. He died in 1979.

George

Net

Ernest Garbutt, known as Net, was born on 20th July 1910. He lived in Great Ayton and worked on farms around that village, for example he worked for Clifford Petch in Little Ayton. According to Agnes Leckenby, he looked like a true Garbutt with fair curly hair. He married Ella Megginson and had three children, John, Eileen and Maureen. He is remembered as a very jovial man, always laughing and joking and a bit of a comedian. He died in 1980.

A final daughter for Isaac and Mary Emma, was Hannah Elizabeth, who was born on 23rd December 1912. She was adopted aged about two and a half by cousin Robert, son of Isaac's sister Elizabeth, and his wife Ada, who lived in Nottingham. In 1921 the family moved to Lincolnshire where Hannah met and married Wilf Welbourn. The couple had three children, Barrie, Ricky and Jane.

During the Second World War Wilf joined the RAF while Hannah worked as a nurse and an ambulance driver. After the war, in 1946, the family moved to Skegness and Hannah ran a small boarding house while Wilf worked as a surveyor for a company which built sea defences for several Lincolnshire towns. After selling the boarding

Hannah

house, Hannah worked first as a domestic science teacher and later as the regional supervisor for school meals. Wilf sadly died just after he retired from his job as a surveyor for agricultural land drainage schemes, and Hannah moved to Nottingham to live with her daughter Jane. She died in 2001.

The final child born to the Garbutts of Wingroves Farm was Joseph Stanley, known as Stan, who was born on 29th April 1917. Stan owned White House Farm, South Broughton, and in 1967 he sold this to buy the shop which included a petrol station and post office, at Chop Gate. He moved from the shop to Stoney Intake, then Hagg End.

Stan

Whilst living in Broughton Stan married Kathy Rose, who already had three children, Sandra, Linda and Brian, from her first marriage. Stan and Kathy later had two daughters, Kathleen and Anne.

Stan was a well known character in Chop Gate area. During the Second World War he served with the Great Broughton Home Guard and he was the village postman for around ten years; as such he became a valued member of the community. Like many of his siblings, he loved horses and enjoyed going to point-to-points and race meetings. He would also rush his post round in order to go fox hunting which was another pastime he enjoyed.

Stan retired to Stokesley in 1980 and was known to say he would be happy if he lived to be "three score year and ten" but sadly he died of a malignant tumour on 28th March 1987 aged 69 years, one month before he reached this milestone.

From this description it is clear that the Garbutts are a close-knit family. Until the early part of the twentieth century few of them had moved more than a few miles from Bilsdale and most of them were involved in agriculture for all or part of their lives. Since then most of the family have moved away from the Dale and few are now involved in farming. At the moment there are 425 direct descendents (621 if one includes spouses) of Robert Garbutt (senior) on his family tree and more are born every year. Of all these people, one has always intrigued me more than any - John William (Jack) Garbutt, the second son of Isaac and Mary Emma, the Bilsdale Bombardier.

Jack

Chapter 2
Life at Wingroves in 1900

The farmhouse known as Wingroves (sometimes spelt Whingroves) was built by Isaac (senior) in the early 1870s. Isaac had taken over the tenancy of the farm at Michaelmas 1861 with a rent of £9 11s 0d from 1861 and then £9 14s 0d from 1865-1868.

The new house was built on the site of an earlier hovel by Isaac and his brother William, who was a stonemason and helped him with the building work. The stones for the house were undressed, but the stable and barn which were built later were made from dressed stones. Roofers from the Feversham estate were brought in to do the roof - the original hovel would have been thatched but the new house was covered with pantile.

According to local tradition, in the years around 1860-1870 the local landowner, Lord Feversham, occasionally offered his tenants incentives in the form of money and materials to build new houses on the land they occupied. Mr Frankland, the occupier of Wingroves from 1953-1987, has discovered that Isaac was offered such a deal and he was paid £3 17s 6d by Lord Feversham to build the new house at Wingroves.

Although the Wingroves farmhouse itself was built in the 1870s, there had been land known by the same name for over two centuries. Surveys of Bilsdale show that in 1637, part of a farm known as Hastybanke was:

> *Halfe of one intack* [a piece of land reclaimed from the moor] *and pasture and arable called Whyngraves containing 8 acres.*[1]

A re-estimation of the land in Bilsdale five years later produced a more accurate picture and in 1642 the tenant of Hastiebancke, Widow Hugall, had an intack called Whingraves of 40 acres 3 roods 30 perches. The value of this portion of land was £3 1s 6d.[2]

At the time of the next survey in 1781, the area known as Whingraves was divided between the two tenancies at Hasty Bank and in 1814 John Coverdale, tenant of Hasty Bank held 41 acres 0 roods 2 perches, presumed to be the same land.[3]

Wingroves Farm with Issac (Junior), Mary Emma, Gladys and Harry taken about 1905

In the 1826 survey John Coverdale is described as "Tenant of Wingraves" with land covering 40 acres 1 rood and 21 perches.[4]

On 22nd September 1913 the property was valued for tax purposes. The size of the farm is given as 41 acres, 0 roods and 21 perches. The owner is given as the Earl of Feversham with Isaac Garbutt named as the occupier. The rent is listed as £13 13s and the farm is on an annual lease starting on Lady Day. The Earl of Feversham is noted as being responsible for repairs and insurance. A full description of the farm is given:

Poor dale farm known as Whin Groves situated at the high end of Bilsdale in a bleak and exposed position. The land is very poor indeed. Stokesley is the nearest market - 5 miles, Ingleby station - 4 miles. Only fair road. There is a good moor stray attached to this farm for 50 sheep but it is not included in this valuation, being valued with the moor. House stone and tiled in just fair repair, contains 2 living rooms, and dairy, 3 bedrooms. Buildings stone and tiled in poor repair.

The farm is valued at £250 with £60 of this being the value of structures on the property.[5]

A plan accompanying this document shows outbuildings belonging to the property - a cow house, fodder store, barn, stable, turf shed, boiler house, 3 pigsties and a cart shed.

The evidence of all of these surveys shows that the basic extent of the farm where Jack Garbutt grew up had changed very little over 270 years. Indeed, when the Feversham estate was divided up and sold in 1944, the area for the Wingroves tenancy was still virtually unchanged at 39.042 acres, although the rent had risen to £23.00.[6] Wingroves was part of the Urra estate which was bought by Mr Jackson, a coal merchant from the Otley area.

Life on this farm would have been tough - probably little more than subsistence farming. The land would have been used for pasture for grazing the cows and sheep and for meadows for cutting hay for the winter. Surplus milk from the cows would have been made into butter by the women of the family who would also have been responsible for looking after the poultry - hens and possibly ducks and geese. A few crops such as turnips and potatoes would have been grown and possibly some oats and corn.

Pigs would have been important on the farm. They would live on the household waste and then in turn be killed to provide food for the family. The meat would be shared amongst neighbours who each took it in turns to kill a pig.[7]

Another feature of the farm would be horses. These would have been medium sized horses (cobs) which were able to deal with the hilly ground. They would have been used for all kinds of tasks on the farm and for going to market, either in harness or being ridden. We can be sure that Jack Garbutt and his brothers would have worked with these animals from a young age.

Bilsdale Horses

Income would have been derived from selling butter, eggs and from selling sheep or their fleeces - either in the Dale or at a market such as Stokesley. It is also possible that livestock or produce was taken to markets further afield on the train. Wingroves was not a long way from Ingleby Greenhow station and distribution and movement was much easier once the railways were relatively accessible.

Bilsdale Weather

The weather would have played a part in making life hard in the Dale. In the Log Book of Bilsdale School[8], the Headmaster often writes about extreme conditions.

For example, in the school year 1903-04, he comments about the weather at least once in nearly every month.

In August the weather was wet:

18th August 1903 - A downpour of rain caused a poor attendance this morning.

29

25th August 1903 - The morning being wet, the attendance was poor.

Similar conditions are mentioned four times in September and October and this must have made it difficult to harvest the corn that year (the school corn harvest holidays were from 16th September to 12th October).

Winter starts early in Bilsdale and on 17th November 1903 the Master wrote:

The weather being snowy and stormy there was a decline in attendance.

In early December things got even worse:

1st December 1903 - In consequence of a snowstorm, only 15 children attended today.

2nd December 1903 - The severe cold weather of today prevented more than 23 children attending.

7th December 1903 - A very stormy day with 12 children in attendance.

It is highly probably that the Garbutt children would not have attended school on days such as these; the journey from Wingroves into the village is approximately three miles on a farm track down a steep hill.

January, February and early March 1904 were also wet and stormy months:

8th February 1904 - A very wet and rough morning - not fit for children living at a distance to be out. Only 22 children present.

2nd March 1904 - Rough and stormy weather; too rough for children living far from school. 22 children present.

By mid-March however, things had started to improve:

18th March 1904 - The weather this week has been fine.

Finally, in May, a different weather problem is apparent:

2nd May 1904 - A high gale is probably the cause of a thin attendance today.

Two years later May was a much more difficult month:

17th May 1906 - The ground was covered with snow.

Such extremes must have made farming a difficult occupation for Bilsdale residents.

Leisure Time

We do not have much evidence relating to how the Garbutts spent any leisure time but there are certain activities in which they are likely to have participated.

For example, we do not know if the family were regular churchgoers, although it is certain that Jack was confirmed and that Gladys was friendly with the daughter of the local Vicar, Mary Flora Parry, who gave her a Bible in 1916. It is therefore possible that at least some of the family attended services, probably at the Church of England Parish Church of St. Hilda's, which was a walk across fields and not as far as it may appear by road. Weddings, funerals and special services for events such as Harvest, Christmas, Easter, Rogation Sunday and Sunday School anniversaries may well have formed part of life for Jack and his family.

Another possible leisure time activity was following the hunt. The Bilsdale Hunt is one of the oldest in England and although active participation would have been beyond the means of the Garbutts, it cost nothing to follow. Jack's youngest brother Stan did this and it is possible that his elder siblings were also involved.

It is almost certain that the Garbutt family would have attended agricultural shows such as the Bilsdale Agricultural Show. This first took place in 1895 and has been a regular event on the last Saturday of August ever since. As well as allowing for relaxation and meeting friends and neighbours, this would also have been an opportunity for the farmers of Bilsdale to show off their talents by exhibiting livestock and produce.

Bilsdale Agricultural Show

Several members of the Garbutt family were quite musical, such as John Garbutt son of Robert (junior) and Mary Emma's mother. Music was also part of Jack's life as he owned a zither; we can only imagine where he learned to play such an unusual instrument!

Apart from this, there was probably little time or energy for other recreation. There were lots of organised activities going on in the Dale - cricket and the Bilsdale Band for example, but it seems unlikely that any of the Wingroves Garbutts would have taken part - it was a long walk down the hill at the end of a hard day at work.

Chapter 3
School Years

Jack started school on 18th June 1902 at the age of six and a half. This was 18 months later than was required by law but starting school late was not unusual in the Garbutt family; Jack's brother Harry was nearly eight and a half before he first attended.[1]

When young children first went to school up until the age of about seven, they were put into the Infant class. They then worked through the "standards" as follows:

Standard I   approximate age 7-8.
Standard II   approximate age 8-9.
Standard III   approximate age 9-10.
Standard IV   approximate age 10-11.
Standard V   approximate age 11-12.
Standard VI   approximate age 12-13.

According to an entry in the school log book for 3rd August 1900, it was normal practice for boys to leave school on their thirteenth birthday.[2]

The Headmaster of the school at the time kept a detailed log[3] and from this we can trace certain events of Jack's school days. For example, he kept a record of what children in the school were studying at the time. A typical scheme of work for a year would be as follows:

Scheme of Instruction for Year Ending 30th June 1904.

Lower Division
English - Standards I and II to read from St. George Historical Reader Book I; New Graphic Reader Book II and

Arnold's Countryside Reader Book I. Standard III to read from Graphic Geographical reader; Stories from English History and King Alfred Reader.
Copy book writing and transcriptions.
Formation of easy sentences both oral and written
Recitation - The Voice of Spring and The Captain by Tennyson.

Arithmetic - scheme B.
Group A as in schedule 1 (Code) for Standard I.
Group B as in schedule 1 (Code) for Standard II.
Group C as in schedule 1 (Code) for Standard III.

Geography - simple lessons in Geography of neighbourhood and outlines of England. Explanation of geographical terms as they occur.

Elementary Science and Common Things - 1. The Turnip 2. Cabbages 3. Carrots 4. Potatoes 5. Onions 6. Grass 7. Parts of a flower 8. Work in the fields in Spring 9. Work in the fields in Summer 10. Work in the fields in Autumn 11. Work in the fields in Winter 12. Rooks and Crows 13. Cultivation 14. The Farm Yard 15. The Dairy 16. The Bee 17. The Frog 18. The Snail 19. The Earthworm 20. The Spider 21. The Sheep 22. The Dog 23. Water 24. Saltwater and Freshwater 25. Evaporation 26. Rain 27. The work of water 28. Clay 29. Sand, sandstone and gravel 30. Soils.

Drawing - simple geometrical forms drawn with a ruler and freehand.
Designs developed from ruler exercises.

Singing - as in appendix IV to revised instructions.

Needlework - as in appendix III to revised instructions.

Physical Education - as in schedule III of the Code.

Upper Division
English - Reading from Ideal Historical Reader Book IV; Geographical Reader on Europe; Buchannan's Country Reader Book I.
Copy book writing. Reproductions of passages from Reading book.
Accounts of familiar objects and scenes. Letter writing. Grammatical rules bearing upon correct composition.

Recitation - The Stag Hunt - Sir W Scott and Songs from The Princess - Tennyson.

Arithmetic - scheme B.
Group A as in schedule 1 (Code) for Standard VI.
Group B as in schedule 1 (Code) for Standard V.
Group C as in schedule 1 (Code) for Standard VI.

Geography - Europe; Map drawing.

Elementary Science and Common Things - as in lower division; children to take notes.

Drawing - as in former codes.

Singing - as in appendix IV to revised instructions.

Needlework - as in appendix III to revised instructions.

Physical Education - as in schedule III of the Code.

From the log books we also know that attendance was not good in the school for a variety of reasons. For example on 13th July 1903 the master wrote:

Several farmers having commenced cutting hay, the attendance has suffered.

Two days later on 15th July 1903 he wrote:

A wet day. Only 20 children in attendance. Register not marked.

However we also learn that the school was shut for things which would not be permitted today such as on 6th July 1903:

Wesleyans has the use of the schoolroom for their annual tea, consequently the children had a holiday.

On one occasion Jack is mentioned by name; on 9th January 1906, the day before his 10th birthday, the log book entry reads:

A wet day; 44 present. Two boys, Robt I and John W Garbutt being wet through were sent home.

One can only imagine what these two boys felt like as they trudged back up the hill to Wingroves, soaking wet, only a short time after walking down to the village in the first place. It is highly probable that Jack was ill with a cold or chill on his birthday.

Various other medical problems which faced the Garbutt family and others in Bilsdale are mentioned several times. For example in July 1907, when Jack was ten, measles was spreading through the Dale with several families affected including the Hoggarts of Clay House, the Dales of Stoney House Court, the Lengs of Ewe

Hill, the Easbys of High West Cote, the Bowes of Staindale and the Garbutts of Wingroves. As a result the school was closed for one month on the advice of the Medical Officer of Health.

We also know that on 16th December 1908, when Jack was 12 and about to leave school on his 13th birthday, illness again struck at Wingroves. The log book entry reads:

> *Mrs Garbutt of Wingroves sent word this morning that all her children were ill in bed and therefore could not attend school.*

A final documented event in Jack's childhood happened on 31st March 1909, when he was confirmed by the Bishop of Beverley at St. Hilda's Church in Chop Gate. This service is noted in the school log book and a small red book entitled *Helps to Worship*, which the local Vicar, the Rev. Parry, presented to Jack to mark the event, still exists.

Although we do not have any other information about Jack's education, we do know a lot about conditions in the school at that time, conditions which can only have affected the education of Bilsdale children in a negative way.

As early as March 1872 an Inspector's report was highlighting the need for additional school places in Bilsdale - 87 places were needed at Chop Gate and 35 at West Side, but only 69 places were actually available. This overcrowding was not alleviated and in 1904, two years after Jack became a pupil, the long fight to have the school rebuilt began.[4]

An Inspector's report of that year notes:

> *Considering that the master is teaching as many children in one smallroom (with no help, except a boy) the results are creditable to him.*
>
> *In one half of the room, which is only 15 feet wide, the long desks are 5 rows deep; the infants are taught in the two front desks and necessarily make poor progress under such conditions.*

The work done by the older children is much better.
There is only one available room for all the children - that room is 15 feet wide and the long desks are 5 rows deep. The walls (stone) are 11 inches thick and are very damp; the floor is rotten and the general condition is so bad that repairing is of little use.

In October 1904 the Board of Education in London decided that the school should be condemned and that the existing premises should not be recognized after 30th June 1906. The condemnation of the school was overwhelming with one Inspector, Mr Holmes, writing:

This is one of the worst cases I have ever had to deal with.

Another inspection report, written by Mr Roberts in June 2005 said:

The school is taught under depressing conditions, there is very little teaching space and the bad lighting must be very injurious to the eyesight of the children.
An assistant served in the school for six months but the master is now single handed with from 50 to 60 children. It is quite impossible to give suitable instruction or employment to the infants and the warning with the last report should be borne in mind.
Great credit is due to the master for the successful teaching of the school. The older children are all well advanced and do particularly good work, although the age at admission is seldom much under six. Better arrangements should be made for regular and frequent cleaning of the classroom and offices [toilets].

In June 1906 the North Riding of Yorkshire LEA submitted plans for provision of out offices and cloakrooms fitted with lavatory basins but these were rejected by Mr Roberts as:

> ...totally unsatisfactory. The essential part of any alteration is the provision of a good schoolroom. The plans leave the main premises untouched. In my opinion any addition of cloakrooms would be a waste of money and mere tinkering. The floor is worn out and the walls so damp that, though coloured at Easter, they appear as if untouched for years. The lighting is bad, the top of the windows 7½ feet high.

At this point the Board of Education in London started to be very critical of the owner of the school building, Lord Feversham, writing:

> Lord Feversham has had to do very little in the last twelvemonth, the amount of work at Harome and Fadmoor, which has had to be pressed for, being trifling in actual amount, a few days work at each place.

It certainly seems to have been acknowledged early that:

> Lord F would only seize the opportunity for further delay.

A further visit to the school in November 1906 by the Board of Education's architect, Mr S R Tatham, resulted in the following report:

> The walls of the existing mixed school room are only 9" thick and they show signs of damp.
> The garden on the south side is about 2' above the level of the floor.
> The heights of the room are insufficient.
> The heating is unsatisfactory.

The floor is in a very bad condition.
There is no proper cloakroom and lavatory accommodation.
The Infants room, which is approached through the mixed schoolroom, was built as part of the Master's house. The walls are thick but the height (10'6") is low, the floor being beneath the level of the ground.
The "double" offices are insufficient and contrary to rule and those used by G and I [girls and infants??] *are common to the inmates of the Master's house. The proposal to build cloakrooms and offices at once and to gradually remodel the rest of the school will not produce a convenient and well-arranged building.*
The intention is to increase the width of the mixed schoolroom, [illegible] *out 2 gables towards the road and to provide a new floor and a new roof, to build a new room for infants with a separate approach and to give back the existing Infants Room to the Master's house.*
An entirely new building should be provided, the rooms being arranged as to secure left side light to the desks and conveniently placed fires.
If the proposals of the managers were carried out there would be very little of the existing school left.

Finally in September 1907, plans were approved for a new school building for not more than 44 mixed and 32 infant scholars. Even now, concerns about Lord Feversham's attitude to the building work were expressed:

Lord F is certain to delay the building of the school as much as possible unless strong pressure is brought to bear upon him.

Therefore in October the Board of Education decided that the grant and recognition of the school would be withheld until assurances were given about the date that the new school premises would be ready for occupation.

In order to resolve the situation, Lord Feversham's estate wrote in October 1907:

> *Lord Feversham ... is quite prepared to commence building the new school at once.... I think I can promise to have it ready for occupation by the end of the summer holidays. The winter is fast approaching and in such a place it is difficult to get a good staff of men to work, but I think we can complete by the time named.*

This proposed deadline of summer 1908 was not met. In October 1908 only the:

> *...offices nearing completion, main building to be proceeded in due course.*

In November 1908 Rev. J. Parry, the local vicar and manager of the school, wrote to the Board of Education that:

> *The managers would have your committee and the Board of Education bear in mind that it is not the nature of things to expect much progress at this season of the year when among these hills the winter is rigorous and when frost and snow often possess the earth for weeks. However we shall do our best in the matter...*

Long debate continued in London that winter as to whether the grant and recognition of the school should be suspended in order to encourage the LEA to keep up the pressure on Lord Feversham. Mr Roberts was finally dispatched to inspect the building works and in December 1908 he wrote:

The offices are not complete. The roof is on and they are being used as a workshop. A little progress has been made with the new walls. Part of the foundations are in, but the serious work of pulling down the old school has not been entered on.

Suspension of the grant has caused the LEA to write strong letters to Lord F (the managers have nothing to do with the matter at all) and if the school is not finished in the early summer, they will, as in the case of Rudland, refuse to maintain it.

If the school is not finished by the summer of 1909 all work will stop as the farmers will be too busy to do the carting. The builder or contractor does no carting, this being a service due from the tenant to the landlord.

Without extreme pressure from the LEA work will not be resumed then till late autumn and the school may not be finished till the spring of 1910. To get the school finished in 1909, I expect that the LEA will have to refuse to maintain and this is a step the Committee will scarcely trouble to take if they think that the Board have ceased to attach importance to the matter, by reversing their plainly expressed intention to pay no further grant till proper buildings are provided.

Later in March 1909 he wrote:

With some difficulty I reached the school today, a storm having laid drifts on the roads in and out.

1. The closets are complete but only half are usable, the urinal is not finished. The classroom walls are finished and the rafters in position but nothing else. Floor and roof both wanting. It will be long before the classroom is fit for use and the serious work of pulling down the old school has not been entered on. Since Xmas the winter has undoubtedly been severe in the dale (a very different place to the moors above) and but for that fact I should consider the progress made since I saw the work on December 24ᵗʰ thoroughly unsatisfactory. Nothing has been done but to raise 3 small walls and put the rafters in position.

2. I certainly think a deduction sought to be made from the grant. I was much impressed today by the atrocious character of the room in which the children work. Unless the rate of progress is very considerably accelerated, there is no prospect whatsoever of the school being completed by 30.6.1909.

It was finally agreed in March 1909 that the grant for year ending 30ᵗʰ June 1908 would be paid with a deduction of three shillings per unit of average attendance. This low reduction was decided because of the weather. The authority was reminded that payment of the current year's grant was conditional on the Board being satisfied that all possible dispatch was used in the erection of the new premises as soon as the weather became favourable to building operations.

In August 1909, questions were again being asked. Mr A Wallis wrote:

I visited the school today work is going on slowly, nothing is finished. The classroom is unpainted, the stone wall requires pointing and the stone coping to the roof is not in place. The offices are practically finished but here the boy's urinal is not complete; it is open to the road and the boys are using a temporary wooden erection in one corner of the playground. The main room is as yet unplastered without a ceiling. The floor is done. There are still 2 or 3 loads of stone to be carted. The girl's cloakroom is partially tiled. There are 2 joiners, a stone mason and 2 boys who help him employed at present. A plasterer is expected to come up soon. The children are being taught in the new and old classroom. At the present rate of work it will take a month or two to get the school done.

The LEA was asked to explain the situation and wrote that month:

... exceptionally wet spring and summer ... cannot complain of the progress of the work. It must be remembered that this is a very isolated place and tradesmen are very scarce and have occasionally to leave the work to attend to other customers. It is also the practice in these parts to cease building operations during the hay harvest to assist farmers and smallholders to get in their crops, and owing to the weather, the hay harvest has been prolonged this summer. Special tradesmen such as plasterers are very difficult to persuade to come and work in such out of the way places. Every care has been taken to see that the children take no harm. Again it has been found very difficult to carry on building and the work of the school at the same time.

Again the question of grant payments arose and in September 1909 the situation was summarized as follows:

The excuses are various e.g. bad weather, shortage of labour, isolated position, school in use during rebuilding. There is no doubt some justice in all these pleas. But the real trouble seems to have been the apathy of Lord Feversham, the owner.

And in September 1909 the North Riding of Yorkshire LEA was informed that the Board of Education was:

... not satisfied that the work has been pressed forward with such expedition as the urgency of the case demanded

... No grant will be paid until the work is satisfactorily completed and the architects certificate received at this office, and that in any case it can not be paid without a very substantial deduction.

The LEA was obviously unhappy with this and replied asking that the grant be paid with no deduction as:

Every possible step has been taken to expedite the completion. The school is private property and the owner is also owner of practically all the land in the district and has done a lot of work in connection with school buildings on his estate.

I therefore hope that your Board will take into consideration the whole of the circumstances of this case and not penalise this authority for what has not been in any way their fault.

There was some better news of the school in November 1909 when an HMI report commented:

The new rooms are both being used for teaching purposes but the larger is not quite finished, there is still some painting to do. The pegs are not fixed in the cloakrooms and the master complains that the presence of workmen on the premises interferes with the instructors. It will be one month, possibly two, before the school is completed, for there is still some stone to be brought and this must be shaped into flags for the front yard. Two masons are now at work in the boy's playground on the ridge stones, and until they have finished, it will hardly be possible to use this playground for physical exercises, nor can the girl's playground be used, for it is a mass of loose stones. There is still some work on the master's house to be done.

An architect's certificate dated 19th November 1909 and signed by Robert P Brotton gave the following dimensions for the new school rooms:

Boys/Mixed Schoolroom	24' x 22'	= 528 square feet.
Classroom	16' x 17'9"	= 284 square feet.
Total		= 812 square feet.

At that time this provided accommodation for the following numbers of students:

Mixed	=	44.
Infants	=	32.
Total	=	76.

Despite the completion of the building works a further grant deduction six shillings per unit of average attendance was made for the school year ending 1909 but not before these final comments were made by officers at the Board of Education:

> Lord Feversham is an exasperating person to deal with but, from what I have seen of the proceedings of the N Riding LEA, I feel sure that they have not taken the best, if any, steps to get the work hurried on.
> We cannot properly pay grants in respect of a school which is conducted in seriously defective premises at a rate equal to that on which grants are calculated in respect of a school in which the premises are satisfactory.

In March 1910 a certificate was granted saying that the school provided accommodation for 44 mixed students and 32 infants. This saga comes to an end, just after Jack's education had finished, with an inspection report from 27th April 1910 signed by A Wallis:

The school is now established in the enlarged premises and for the first time the teachers are able to work under proper conditions. It is greatly to the credit of the master that he has successfully carried on the work during the constant disturbance caused by the prolonged building operations.

The school is energetically taught and the children are well-behaved, interested in their work and generally intelligent. The work reaches a satisfactory level. Composition is well done in the upper part of the school. Geography is interestingly taught and the children use their atlases, though they might be taught to get more information from these and to answer more fully and connectedly. The older and more advanced children should not work all the time with Standards IV and V. The necessary books, with the exception of a History text book are available for them to prepare some of their work suitably.

The children in the lower group, Standards I - III, should do more of their arithmetic mentally and be expected to make clear statements about their sums. At present they do not talk so freely or audibly as the infants who are being well-taught by the Pupil-Teacher in the main room under the supervision of the Headmaster.

Premises - the school buildings are at last quite finished though there are workmen about at odd times, pointing the playground wall.

Full grant might, I think, be paid from the date of Inspection.

With all this adversity at school level - poor conditions, building work, lack of money due to grants not being paid and so on - as well as the fact they often started school much later than expected, it is perhaps no wonder that some of the Garbutt children of Wingroves did not always become very proficient in the basic skills of reading, writing and arithmetic.

Chop Gate School about 1939 showing the buildings completed in 1910

Chapter 4
1914-1915 The Great Adventure

The War Begins

Jack's great adventure started sometime in the autumn of 1914. The First World War began at the end of July that year when first Austria, Russia then Germany declared war and mobilised their troops. Great Britain declared war on Germany on 4th August following the German invasion of Belgium. Around six million troops would be mobilised across Europe that month.[1]

The mood that summer was very enthusiastic and optimistic; no-one seemed to believe that the war would last very long and everyone expected that it would be all over by Christmas.

The German plan, called the Schlieffen plan, was to invade through Belgium and conquer France within six weeks, thus allowing them to concentrate on fighting on the Eastern Front. However the Belgians resisted the advance as strongly as possible and gained some time for the French and British to mobilise. The British Expeditionary Force (BEF) sailed to France and was first involved in battle on 23rd August at Mons. The British had only just arrived in France and were not ready for battle so it not surprising that they were forced to retreat along with their French allies.

This retreat lasted two weeks until 4th September. By this time, the German advance was faltering; the army's logistics were overstretched so that getting supplies, ammunition and so on to the front line was difficult, and 100,000 troops had to be diverted to the Russian front. The French and British counterattacked in the Battle of the Marne and succeeded in pushing the Germans back as far as the River Aisne. It was at this point that troops first began to dig the trenches for protection against snipers and shells. That this would not be a war of movement was confirmed after the first Battle of Ypres in October/November 1914. During this battle, the "Race to the Sea" had ended with the Allies keeping control of the channel ports after the Belgians flooded their own territory by opening the sluice gates at Nieuport. However, the Germans soon launched further attacks near Ypres and, although the Allies defended this town, they were unable to push the enemy back any further. By the end of the year casualties were already high, and trenches, which would be home to both sides for the next four years, stretched from the Channel to the Alps.

Soon after the War began it became clear that many more troops would be needed. The BEF, which had been about 100,000 strong in August 1914, had lost 16,200 men who were killed, 47,707 wounded and 16,746 missing or taken prisoner; it had virtually been wiped out.[2]

Jack Volunteers

Jack had already left Bilsdale by the start of the War. We know that sometime around 1912-13 he was working for a Mr Robinson at West House Farm, Foxton near Sedgefield. Interestingly this farm is only about a mile away from Heley House where Jack's younger brother Harry settled in 1939. After this, probably around January 1914 when he celebrated his 18th birthday, he moved to Hartlepool, a town at a distance of about 25 miles from Bilsdale, where he worked as a policeman alongside his brother Bob.

All around the country, from the first days of the war, men went to their local recruiting offices to enlist. Jack was the only one of the Garbutt brothers to serve and he did not have to enlist that early as there was no conscription at the time. He was also too young; the age at which one could officially join up for service overseas was 19 but Jack was only 18.

We know that Jack enlisted in West Hartlepool in the early Autumn of 1914. The 21st Division which he joined was formed during that time mainly from men from the north of England and Lincolnshire.[3] This was New Army Division - one which was only formed after the outbreak of the War.

Why did Jack join the army? We cannot be sure of course; perhaps he was filled with patriotic fervour and the desire to do his bit for Britain or he could see an opportunity to do something a bit more exciting with his life, to see a bit of the world beyond Bilsdale. The most likely possibility (one supported by memories of his siblings) is that a group of friends was also enlisting and he didn't want to be left behind.

Once he had "taken the King's Shilling" he returned home and a few days later he received his joining instructions and travel warrant.

Jack in 1914

Jack had enlisted in the Royal Field Artillery and became Gunner 63978 in C Battery of the 96th Brigade, part of the 21st Division. As a Gunner Jack would have earned one shilling, two and a half pence per day.[4] In the 21st Division there were four artillery brigades, the 94th, 95th, 96th and 97th, and Jack was to serve with three of these during the War.

It is likely that he chose this regiment due to his experience with horses as these were in greater use in the artillery compared to the infantry. The large numbers of horses needed for a division can be seen in the table on page 53 and at the outbreak of war the supply of horses for the whole army was raised from 25,000 to 165,000. By June 1915 the army had, in effect, conscripted 8% of heavy horses and 25% of saddle horses previously in use on farms.[5] More were acquired (up to a peak of 591,324 horses and 231,149 mules in 1917) as the size of the army increased.[6] Many of these horses and mules were bought in the normal way but others were commandeered; 275,097 were bought and shipped over from Canada and the USA, 7,500 from South America and 3,700 from Spain and Portugal.[7] They were trained for up to six weeks before being transported to the battlefields. So many horses served on the Western Front that one quarter of all shipping from Britain to France during the War carried fodder for horses and this was the heaviest single item transported across the channel, even when compared to ammunition.[8] Most of the horses were used not by the cavalry, but for pulling guns or wagons in the days before mass use of motor vehicles - in August 1914 the Army Service Corps had just 507 motor vehicles although by January 1918 it had 22,000 trucks in France alone.[9] The welfare of horses was the responsibility of the Army Veterinary Corps and it is worth highlighting that over 260,000 horses and mules were destroyed or killed during the war and many others were wounded or gassed.

Table 1 - Organisation of a Division in 1914[10]

	Numbers	Details
Division	18,000 men 5000 horses	Usually commanded by a Major General. Consisted of: Divisional Headquarters 3 Infantry Brigades **3 Royal Field Artillery Brigades** 1 Howitzer Brigade 1 Heavy Artillery of the Royal Garrison Artillery 1 Divisional Ammunition Column 3 Royal Engineer Field Companies 3 Companies of the Army Service Corps (for Transport) 3 Field Ambulances from the Royal Army Medical Corps Veterinary sections from the Army Veterinary Corps Divisional Signal Company from the Royal Engineers Divisional Cyclist Company Mounted Troops
Artillery Brigade	795 men 748 horses	Usually commanded by a Lieutenant- Colonel. Consisted of: Brigade Headquarters **3/4 Batteries** Ammunition Column
Battery	198 men 4/6 guns	Usually commanded by a Major, Captain (second-in-command) 3 Lieutenants or Second-Lieutenants 193 others - see page 54

To help understand the size of a division, it is interesting to note that when in formation it covered 15 miles of road and took seven hours to pass a given point.[11]

The personnel of an Artillery battery would include:

> *A Battery Sergeant-Major , a Battery Quartermaster Sergeant, a Farrier-Sergeant, 4 Shoeing Smiths (of which 1 would be a Corporal), 2 Saddlers, 2 Wheelers, 2 Trumpeters, 7 Sergeants, 7 Corporals, 11 Bombardiers, 75 Gunners, 70 Drivers and 10 Gunners acting as Batmen.*[12]

Jack's battery worked with 18 pounder guns. These had been introduced in 1904 and were robust, accurate guns with a range of 6,525 yards. They fired shrapnel shells, first used at the end of the eighteenth century and named after their inventor Lieutenant Henry Shrapnel RA. These shells comprised a steel casing with 375 lead balls inside which were timed to burst in mid-air, about 20 feet above and in front of its target, scattering its marble sized balls over a wide area.[13] They were mainly

18-pounder gun in action: Western Front 1917. (IWM Q.5811)

used to cut wire or attack troops in the open. Another type of ammunition, high explosive shells, which were introduced just after the start of the war and developed greater accuracy over the course of the next four years, were used to attack solid targets such as dugouts. Each gun was pulled by a team of six horses, and other horses pulled limbers of shells to the guns from the ammunition dumps behind the lines. This was a mammoth task - in June 1916 each gun had 1,000 rounds ready at its position at any time and by the summer of 1917, 18 pounders could use up to one million rounds per week.[14]

Artillery limber bringing up ammunition, July 1916 (IWM Q.4063)

Each field gun was manned by a crew of men. The make-up of the team varied but typically would consist of:

    № 1 - the Commander.
    № 2 - who operated the breech lever.
    № 3 - the 'Layer', who adjusted the sights, signalled adjustments to the No 1 and fired the gun.
    № 4 - the 'Loader'.
    № 5 - passed ammunition to the No. 4 and checked the fuses.
    № 6 - the second-in-command who set the fuses.[15]

The guns were usually positioned around two miles behind the front line and two or three miles further back were found the wagon lines. Here would be located the horses, wagons and administrative staff and they were places of comparative comfort and relative safety, usually with huts and dugouts for officers and men and hard standing for the horses. Subalterns and gunners would be rotated between the guns and the wagon lines.[16]

The War Diaries and Jack's Letters

Although we have little documentary evidence of events in Jack's life from his confirmation in March 1909 until December 1914, thereafter we have a virtually day-by-day account of what he did and where he was, often down to a precise map reference. This is thanks to two things: Jack's letters to or from his family and the official war diaries kept by his brigade or divisional commanders throughout the war.

Nearly 50 letters which Jack sent survive along with a few letters sent by other people concerned about his welfare; they were found recently amongst the papers of his brother Stan, along with many family photographs and other souvenirs. Transcripts of all these letters are to be found at the end of each chapter. Given what has already been said about the education of the Bilsdale Garbutts, it is interesting to see in these letters, which are all transcribed exactly as in the original document, evidence of a lack of proficiency in spelling and punctuation. However, it is also evident that Jack's literacy skills improved through the course of the war perhaps due to the fact that he was writing letters much more frequently than before he enlisted.

The war diaries of the brigades in which Jack served are now kept at The National Archives in Kew, London. These vary in the amount of detail given and are not always complete, but it is fortunate that the diary for the 94th Brigade, in which

Jack served from August 1916, is unusual in that it not only lists events and map references, but it also contains names of every man wounded or killed throughout the war. The diary transcripts for each year of the war are also found at the end of the relevant chapter.

As a result of these documents we have detailed information about Jack's training. Volunteers at the time had on average a ten month training period[17], and we know that by the end of the year Jack had travelled south, to the area around Tring in Hertfordshire where the 21st Division was based. He spent the winter months training at camps like the one now known as RAF Halton. In 1914 this belonged to Mr Alfred Rothschild, of the famous banking family, who had inherited the estate in 1879. When volunteers started joining the army in the autumn of 1914, Alfred Rothschild was one of the first landowners to offer land to be used for training camps and around 20,000 men came to Halton, to live in tents through an increasingly muddy winter as they completed their training.[18]

Postcard from Berkhamstead

By May 1915 Jack was billeted at the home of Mrs Hibble at 12 Holliday Street, Berkhamsted with George, another soldier from his battery. He had some leave, probably in early May 1915, and when he returned to his billet he brought with him some eggs from Wingroves which were much appreciated:

> *The land lady thanks you very much for those eggs she thinking about sending for a few more she says we cant get eggs like those down here.*[19]

He also took part in firing a volley over the grave of Herbert Sykes, a member of his battery, who died on 22nd May 1915:[20]

> *Driver Scykes in our battery got killed the other week and their was a military funeral at hemel-hemstead, and I was one of the firing party to fire three volleys over his grave. Poor fellow I was sorroy for him when I saw the acident occurred. We had just been changing the horses for him that afternoon when it occurred. They were six fresh horses. I should think the had never been in a waggon before, and as soon as they got them yoked and mounted they set off full gallop across the park. The lead driver jumped down from his horse and let them go, and they pulled the centre drivers horse down, and poor sykes was trampled over with the horses and the two wheels went over his chest and broke his chest in. He belonged to Doncaster.*[21]

Jack was involved in escorting prisoners around the country in the summer of 1915 and as a result travelled to Northampton and Stratford; as he said in a letter to his parents:

> *I am getting a few looks round the country.*[22]

The men did a lot of route marching and temperatures that summer were very hot causing a great deal of suffering:

> *The heat is very powerful down here now, it fair scorches us. The infantry men as something to put up with when they are marching, they have 22 pounds to carry on their backs. One day when they were out marching last week it was pitiful to see the poor beggers laid by the road-side. Some were carried on stretchers, some were unconcious, and others died after it, so that will give you an idea what the heat is like down here. We have it a lot better than they have we ride nearly three-parts of the way.[23]*

On 2nd July, Jack's brigade moved to Milford in Surrey and during this time he travelled to Stonehenge from where he sent a postcard home. While at Milford the men slept under canvas and based on a letter which Mrs Hibble sent to Mary Emma, rations deteriorated:

> *they were only having 2 meals a day when they have been having in Billets 4 good meals.[24]*

After his training period, Jack left for France on 10th September 1915 when he moved from Milford to Southampton from where he sailed to Le Havre in Normandy, France, arriving on 11th September. Over the next 15 days, Jack's unit travelled by train and on foot for over 200 miles to Loos, near Lens in northern France. They arrived on 25th September and it was here, at the Battle of Loos, that Jack would experience combat for the first time. Sometime on this journey Jack went to a YMCA canteen and used some of their writing paper to send a letter to his parents. He sounds like much of the propaganda of the time when thinking about his forthcoming first taste of action:

Well it will be the first time in action for us, and I hope we shall warm their jackets, whip them out of this country, Belgium and across Germany to Berlin. Do not get worried about me as I shall be alright here with my brave Pals.[25]

The Battle of Loos

The bombardment for this attack, which was part of a joint offensive with France, started on 21st September and continued continuously for four days and nights until the main assault began on 25th September. The 21st Division was held in reserve but Jack would have been able to hear the bombardment and know that war was near. On 25th September the fighting divisions made good progress; gas was used by the British Army for the first time and a potential break in the German lines opened up. At this point the reserve divisions, were called into action. Martin Middlebrook comments that the 21st Division (and 24th Division) had been chosen for this task because they were:

Fresh and not burdened with the lethargy of trench holding.[26]

However this is a euphemism for completely inexperienced and it is now clear that the 21st Division was at a real disadvantage: the troops had only recently arrived in France; they had marched approximately 14 miles in the two days (through rain) before going into action; they were tired and hungry as supplies had been slow to get through; their last base was too far back behind the lines.

When the men in reserve were called to advance on 26th September, they arrived too late to take full advantage of the breakthrough of the previous day. General Haig wrote on 29th September:

No reserve was placed under me... They came on as quick as they could poor fellows, but only crossed our old trench line with their heads at 1800 hours. We had captured Loos 12 hours previously and reserves should have been at hand then.[27]

Casualties among the reserve divisions were high; Jack's brigade was luckier than most and did not suffer very high losses with one man killed and six wounded in the last four days of September 1915, but in the nearby 94th Brigade, three men were killed, 13 wounded, two gassed and 11 horses were killed on 26th September alone.[28]

The reserve divisions did have some short-lived success before being pushed back by counter-attacks from the Germans, who were better organised, had more plentiful ammunition and better machine-gun tactics.[29] In the end the battle dragged on without any real gain on either side until early November.

After the battle the 21st and 24th Divisions were seen as having disgraced the good name of the British army.[30] Later however it was realised that the fault lay mainly with officers; the overall commanders had held the reserve too far back from the front line and officers of the new divisions were too inexperienced for active combat. As a result of this, new inexperienced officers were exchanged with more experienced colleagues so that effective command could be ensured.

The new Commander of the 21st Division was David "Soarer" Campbell. He had been given the nickname from the name of his horse, The Soarer, which he had ridden to victory in the 1896 Grand National. He had also won the Irish National Hunt Cup and the Grand Military Steeplechase on other horses and is the only rider to have achieved this treble. Campbell put this equestrian prowess into good use in the army and at the start of the First World War he led some of the last cavalry charges in British military history and was one of the last British soldiers to be wounded by a lance.[31]

According to Richard Holmes, Major General Campbell:

> ...*restored its* [the 21st Division's] *battered morale and commanded it with distinction for the rest of the war, combining frequent visits to the front with personal aerial reconnaissance.*[32]

Jack's brigade had been relieved early in October and the diary records that the men marched 25 miles to Hazebrouck and, after a few days, a further 17 miles to Armentières where they spent the rest of 1915. Although Jack moved in and out of the front line area, he was not part of any major offensive; the New Army Divisions were given some time to regroup after their first experience of the Great War. He was engaged in some minor local action, for example on 15th December when his brigade was involved in a bombardment to destroy enemy positions prior to an infantry attack. However, even these skirmishes could result in heavy casualties; during the operation, C Battery was attacked and a 4.2 shell landed on top of one of the gun emplacements slightly damaging the gun, killing three gunners and wounding the gun commander and two gunners. Jack was a member of C Battery, but we have no way of knowing if he was one of the wounded men. The following day Jack's Battery was sent to rest for 10 days at the corps rest area near Bailleul. During this time Jack received a parcel from home with a cake baked by Mary Emma, but in general the rest does not seem to have been totally welcome:

> *We were only they 10 days and we new it. I should have sooner have been in action 20 times over. We were up to the knees in nothing else but mud.*[33]

As the year came to an end, orders were received about how the 21st Division were to celebrate Christmas. On 23rd

December, the Senior Supply Officer drew half a pound of Christmas pudding per man from the rail head to be issued for consumption on Christmas Day.[34] Following events in December 1914 when a truce had been observed on some parts of the line, a confidential memo was sent on 24th December 1915 to the artillery brigade commanders:

> *The Army Commander has expressed a wish that fire will not be opened up by us on Christmas Day. It is to be clearly understood however that the Germans must not be allowed to take liberties and that, if fire is opened by them, the usual forms of retaliation must be employed.*
>
> *The Army Commander has sent a Christmas Card wishing the Divisional Artillery a Happy Christmas.[35]*

Finally, on 31st December at midnight, Lieutenant-Colonel RC Coates, the Commander of the 96th Brigade wrote:

> *Midnight - we wish the reader of this Diary a more pleasant ending to the coming year, although he may be more favourably situated than we are at present.[36]*

The reader (higher ranking officers at HQ) would surely have been "more favourably situated" to see in the New Year but the situation for all would certainly not be more pleasant in the months ahead.

Artillery Christmas Card, 1915

Letters 1914-15

1. Postcard from Jack to Mary Emma [December 23rd 1914? or possibly earlier]

Dear Mother

I now take pleasure in sending you a card to remind you of your Birthday, and I wish you many happy returns, and I wish you all a merry Christmas and a happy New year, from your ever loving Son

John XXXXX

2. Letter from Mary Emma to Jack [December 23rd 1914] Wingroves Farm, Bilsdale Stokesley

Dear Jack

Just a line to wish you a Merry Xmas and happy New Year am sending you a card little Hannah was 2 year old today I hope you are keeping well Bob was up for the day on Wednesday he does not like his job at Hartlepool what did you think of the bombardment wasent it dreadful you will be getting a card from Bob look out of the 10th of next month if all is well. do drop us just a line Bob says he cant get a word from you he brought your byke home with him so I am taking every care of her for you so now dear Jack I must conclude by sending all our love & best wishes for a Merry Xmas and a happy New Year & Believe Me Always Your Loving Mother

M. E. Garbutt

3. Letter from Jack to Mary Emma and Isaac [May/June 1915?]

96th Brigade RFA, Berkhamsted, Herts,
12 Holliday St

Dear Mother and Father

   just a few lines to let you know that I got back down here alright. It was just one o'clock in the morning, so I had a few hours in bed. The land lady thanks you very much for those eggs she thinking about sending for a few more she says we cant get eggs like those down here. They is a big inspection here tomorrow. We all have to be examined again. Driver Scykes in our battery got killed the other week and their was a military funeral at hemel-hemstead, and I was one of the firing party to fire three volleys over his grave. Poor fellow I was sorroy for him when I saw the acident occurred. We had just been changing the horses for him that afternoon when it occurred. They were six fresh horses. I should think the had never been in a waggon before, and as soon as they got them yoked and mounted they set off full gallop accross the park. The lead driver jumped down from his horse and let them go, and they pulled the centre drivers horse down, and poor sykes was trampled over with the horses and the two wheels went over is chest and broke his chest in. He belonged to Doncaster. I think that is all I can mention this time from your loving Son

   J. W. Garbutt xx

Driver Herbert Sykes, age 19, C Battery, 96th Brigade RFA, died 22.5.1915. Buried in Hemel Hempsted (Heath Lane) cemetery, plot UA 13

4. Letter from Jack to Mary Emma and Isaac [Early Summer 1915?]

Mrs Hibble, 12 Holliday St, Berkhamsted, Herts,

Dear Mother and Father

just a few lines in answering your last letter, hoping this one will find you alright as it leaves me at present. I should have wrote a letter when I was at Northampton but I had not much time so I just sent you a Post Card. I had to escote a prisoner down their to the cells for 2 days. Its a nice place is Northampton. I have to go to Stratford to morrow with one so I am getting a few looks round the country. I think when we shift from here we are going to Milford in Surrey. We are getting a lot of route marching now nearly all the division and theys a nice stretch of us when we are all together. Their is nearly 25 thousand in a division. The heat is very powerful down here now, it fair scorches us. The infantry men as something to put up with when the are marching, they have 22 pounds to carry on their backs. One day when they were out marching last week it was pitiful to see the poor beggers laid by the road-side. Some were carried on stretchers, some were unconcious, and others died after it, so that will give you an idea what the heat is like down here. We have it a lot better than they have we ride nearly three-parts of the way. Well I think that is all this time from your loving Son

     J. W. Garbutt xx

How is little Hannahs eye getting on, I hope it is alright

5. Postcard from M E Hibble to Mary Emma [8ᵗʰ July 1915]

Dear Mrs Garbutt

I cannot understand why Jack or the other fellow have not written they have been gone a week today (Friday) ane there am letters for them to I really think they might write I should feel much easier as I am naturally anxious about them if you have heard *[illegible]* ask Jack not to forget me. Yours Truly ME Hibble

6. Part Letter from M E Hibble to Mary Emma [Summer 1915]

My Dear Mrs Garbutt

Just a line in answer to your most beautiful and welcome letter you don't know how much your letter cheer me Friday for Dear Jack had been gone long before I received your letter I cannot forget him and I hope he write to me we have framed his photo in a frame which my husband made in fretwork it has a soldier on and he his blowing a bugle and the word on it are He Answered His Countrys call and we have Jack in the middle and every time I see it I feel very sad for I so took to Jack and he was so affectionate and I Hope he will write to me but still I know he does not care about writing much I am patiecely waiting and watching every post Jack and I had come very happy hours and good romp very often the other fellow was not much and I don't miss him like Jack they never hardly went out together for Jack was a home bird and He was very steady well my dear Mrs Garbutt I hope you and your husband & family are quite well I am sure it seem very hard for me to part with Jack So what it was for you to part with such a dear lad must have been terrible I hope he will prosper & come back safe and I am sure he will do His duty and God will Help Him & comfort him in all his trials I miss him at chapel for he went with me when I went well my dear I thank you for your letter well my dear if you have Heard from Jack send me His address I though I would send you a line saying he was at Milford camp ...

7. Part letter from M E Hibble to Mary Emma [Summer 1915]

... when I had my dinner yesterday I said I wonder what Jack & George are Having for there dinners well my dear I hope they will like there new life for under canvas they will have to do all for there selves I was in Hopes they would have put them under canvas here because I told them if they were here I could have them to tea now and again and done there washing & mending for them but of course it is not there wish they have to go where they are told I cannot get no news from my brothers I think I have said all this time trusting you are all well I live in Hopes to see you all some day I must try and save up to come & see you all give my love to Jack when you write Remembering yourself & family best love and kisses to all
  believing me to be
          Yours Very Sincerely
                Mary E Hibble

God Bless you & comfort you in parting with such a dear Son for the sake of the Country I feel sure Jack is very good Son for he has such a nice face and ways

8. Letter from M E Hibble to Mary Emma [Summer 1915]

12 Holliday St
Gt Berkhamst Hert

My Dear Mrs Garbutt

I am thinking you will think I am very unkind in not writing before but I have been very ill next to death's door last Thursday I am sure dear one may lay & die when you have no one I am sure if the neighbours next door had been out I should have lay'd & died for we are two cottage to ourselves well I may tell dear Jack has written me a nice letter and of course they have sent me theirs Photos I can assure you my heart bleeds for them because after having such good living and good beds they must feel it terrible I could have cryed when I heard they were only having 2 meals a day when they have been having in Billets 4 good meals I know if any thing happen to my 2 Boys I can always think I have done my part by them for both of us waited on Jack & George & I worked very hard for them and I would again if they came to me for a weekend Jack dear Boy he said he wish he was Back with us I am sending the local paper to Jack telling him to read about the farmers claiming the men. And when my Husband get some good work or some better weeks I am going to send them some cakes & things between them both being as they are in the same Battery I cannot send one and not the other I make no difference between I can say I always treated them both alike but none the more for that Jack was the best of the two and I always call them the boys in talking so I hope you will not mind and there the bed room and there for them whenever they care to come so I cannot speak any fairer can I well I hope your little girl is better I wish Jack had brought her back he said she wanted to come. Hope you & your family are quite well & happy I should love to pop at

Milford poor lads never mind God is good and I am sure he will look after your Son & protect him under his care I know what it is as my Husband was in the RFA and it was through that what has made him suffer so he was discharged last November and has practically not doe anything since then he was in hospital 9 week and I had him at home 3 month all since August 1st he was in Scotland when the war broke out at Camp so you can see what a trying time I have had but I hope my luck will change some day Well my dear I think I will draw to a close trusting at all to One above to help us through this terrible time so will ring of till next time love and kisses

  I remain

      Yours sincerely

         M E Hibble

xxxxxxxxx

Excuse my writing as I am rather weak after lying in bed
Such a lovly letter from jack

9. Post Card (of Stonehenge) from Jack [Summer 1915?]

from Jack

  I will let you know when I am coming shortly we will be abroad in September xxx

  Good Night

10. Letter from Jack to Mary Emma and Isaac [September 1915?]

YMCA - On Active Service with the British Expeditionary Force 1915

Dear Mother and Father

   just a few lines to let you know that I am getting on alright in France. We arrived safe on Saturday morning. Well I expect we shall be in action by the time you get this letter. Don't forget my Address, Gnr _____ 63978 C Batty, 96 Bde RFA, 21 Division, BEF, France. Well it will be the first time in action for us, and I hope we shall warm their jackets, whip them out of this country, Belgium and across Geramany to Berlin. Do not get worried about me as I shall be alright here with my brave Pals. I get on fairly well with the French people they want a bit of understanding but I can manage them alright. I hope you all are keeping well, and Ed pulls through his operation alright. You might write and tell my relations where I am, as I haven't got much time to write to them yet. Well I hope this letter will reach you safely as I know you will have been waiting an answer. Well I dont think their is any think else this time, with all my love and kisses to all from your loving Son

   J.W. Garbutt xx

         Good night and God Bless
                  Till I come home again

11. Letter from Hannah, Ada and Bob to Jack [22nd Dec 1915]

61 Ena Avenue
Sneiton Dale
Nottingham

Dear Cousin Jack

Just a few lines to let you know we got your letter this morning, also the lovely Christmas card you sent us. We were delighted to hear from you. It is very busy just now on the railway and I can hardly get a minute to spare but I promise your Jack that as soon as Xmas is over I will write you a real long letter. Hannah is growing a big bonny girl, very intelligent and nightly before she goes to bed she prays for her brother Jack I have been attested under Lord Derby's group scheme and am in the last group but one on account of my age. Nearly all railwaymen of the eligible ages have been attested. Well jack, our best wishes are for your welfare and may your return safe and sound to Old England be speedy. May God protect you night and day. The card enclosed from Hannah has her name written by herself guided by my hand. A Merry Xmas, Happy New Year be yours. With love from Hannah, Ada and Bob

96th Brigade RFA, War Diary 1915
September 1915; Lt Colonel RC Coates

(For details of notes and abbreviatons please see page 250)

Date

10	MILFORD 2am - 96th Brigade left MILFORD. SOUTHAMPTON 4pm - arrived at docks.
11	HAVRE 10.30am - arrived in port and proceeded to No 5 Camp HAVRE.
12	2.30pm - entrained for ST OMER.
13	ST OMER 10.40am - arrived and left immediately for TOURNEHEM. TOURNEHEM 4.30pm - arrived in billets.
14	At TOURNEHEM.
15	8am - left for WATTEN and there to STAPLES.
16	STAPLES 9am - left for ST JANNS CAPPEL. 3.30pm - arrived.
17	9 officers accompanied by signalers and gunners left for firing line - attached to 12th Division at NIEPPE for experience.
18-19	Exercise, gun drill and signaling practice.
20	Eve - the 9 officers and signalers returned to Brigade.
21	8am - left for METEREN, where Brigade joined remainder of Divisional Artillery. Continued march through MERVILLE and BUSNES LA MIQUELLERIE. 3.45pm - arrived.
22	9.30am - left for BAS RIEUX. 11.15am - arrived.
23	BAS RIEUX 8.30am - wagon lines moved in order to obtain cover from aeroplanes. Orders received to draw 152 rounds of HE ammunition.
24	10.30am - left for direction of firing line.
25	HAILLICOURT 4.30am - arrived and bivouacked. 10.30am - left bivouack for NOEUX LES MINES.

3.30pm - arrived and bivouacked.

7.30pm - left for firing line. Halted for one hour behind Fosse No 3 de BETHUNE, continued march to a point on BETHUNE - LENS road and took up positions for Batteries and Ammunition Column about 11.30pm.

26 Supporting 15th and 21st Divisional Infantry. 388 rounds fired at various objectives.

6pm - positions of Batteries moved slightly forward.

27 FOSSE No 7 de BETHUNE 8am - Batteries and HQ all moved up to positions in front of and to the south of Fosse No 7 de BETHUNE. Lt Col RC COATES temporarily took over command of 21st Divisional Artillery. Major MCGOWAN temporarily took over command of 96th Brigade RFA. 454 rounds fired on Hill 70, BENIFONTAINE and HULLOCH. Casualties - OR 1 killed, 3 wounded. B Battery heavily shelled for a short time.

28 Supporting 2nd Guards Brigade (Gen PONSONBY). Casualties - OR 1 wounded. Rounds fired - 510.

29 In action most of the day Casualties - OR 1 wounded. Rounds fired - 387.

30 In action most of day. Rounds fired - 150. Casualties - 0.

October 1915

1 FOSSE no 7 de BETHUNE In action most of day.

7pm - one section of each Battery relieved by one section of each Battery of 63rd Brigade RFA, 12th Division. Casualties - OR 1 wounded. Rounds fired - 80.

2 B, C & D Batteries heavily shelled. Remaining section of each Battery relieved by remaining section of 63rd Brigade RFA. Rounds fired - 308. Casualties - 2/Lt O'NEILL wounded.

8pm - left position and concentrated behind FOSSE No7 de BETHUNE.

10pm - left for MAZINGARBE.

12 midnight - arrived outside MAZINGARBE village. During the whole of the above fight the Brigade was under the command of Gen WARDROP. The communication to liaison officers with Infantry and also to OPs was extremely difficult owing to lack of wire and to what wire there was being continually cut. Col COATES, i/c 21st Divisional Artillery, arranged with 21st Division, after endless troubles, to have operators and wire attached from signal section for these operations. It is most essential that a section of Divisional Signal Company should be always attached to Divisional Artillery as the Brigades and Batteries have more than they can do to link up with Infantry and their own OPs, all of which lines must be at least duplicated. Runners for communication were very valuable.

3 MAZINGARBE 8.30am - left for NOEUX LES MINES.
NOEUX LES MINES 9.30am - arrived and bivouaked.

4 5.30am - left for MERVILLE.
10.30am - arrived in billets.

5 10.45am - left for HAZEBROUCK.
HAZEBROUCK 2.30pm - arrived in billets. Col COATES returned to command of 96th Brigade. Major MCGOWAN to D/96th.

6 At HAZEBROUCK near HONDEGHEM.

7 7.45am - right section of Batteries with Colonel and Adjutant left for ARMENTIERES where they took over positions from 1st Northumbrian Brigade (50th Division).

8 7.40am - HQ (Brigade) and Brigade Ammunition Column left for ARMENTIERES arriving at 2pm at LA NIEPPE. HQ proceeded to PONT DE NIEPPE - signalers going on to CHAPELLE D'ARMENTIERES.

9 ARMENTIERES 7.40am - left section of Batteries left HAZEBROUCK district for ARMENTIERES relieving left sections of 3rd Northumbrian Brigade (50th Division).

Noon - 96th Brigade HQ took over from the 3rd Northumbrian Brigade. Supporting in trenches 149th and 150th Brigade under Generals BUSH and CLIFFORD respectively and came under tactical command of General HENSHAWE, GOCRA 50th Division. At the time General HOLIDAY 104th Divisional Artillery (23rd Division) was on our right.

10-12 Registering on German trenches and retaliation points. Testing and readjusting telephone communications - arranging FOO positions - getting in touch with Infantry Brigadiers and battalion and trench commanders.

13 2pm - wire cutting by D/96 interrupted by premature display of smoke from Infantry trenches - light was bad and strands of wire were most difficult to observe from a distance of about 400 yards although general effect seemed good and knife-rests seemed badly broken. A,B & C Batteries cooperated firing on enemy trenches and retaliation points. Very little enemy reply.

14 2.30pm - same operation on a minor scale. Enemy reply even less than on previous day. Wagon lines have been completed brick standings for horses and harness rooms. I should like to record our thanks to 3rd Northumbrian Brigade for the excellent gun pits they have made and also for the work they must have done in the wagon lines, in the way of brick standings for horse lines. Their telephonic communication which they left behind for us were also very good.

15-30 Nothing of importance happened beyond daily registration of dumps and possible gun positions which had not already been registered. Wet weather having set in, it was found that considerable alterations had to be made to cover of gun pits handed over by 50th Divisional Artillery as these were in almost every case leaking badly. Owing to the broad span and weight overhead, the roofs had sunk in towards the middle thus preventing the water from draining off.

November 1915; ARMENTIERES

1 On our right is the 23rd Division and on left the 25th Division. Holding the line in front of ARMENTIERES. Immediately on right is the 104th Brigade RFA commanded by Col HOLIDAY and on left is the 95th Brigade RFA commanded by Lt Col FITZGERALD.

4 Capt RDM KEATE (O/C C Battery) was returned to UK.

7 Lieut G TRINTE-DALTON was ordered to join this Brigade.

9 11am - Lt TRINTE-DALTON joined and took over command of C Battery. B Battery slightly shelled; one OR wounded.

 3pm - C Battery heavily shelled; three OR wounded.

 4pm - D Battery heavily shelled; one gun slightly damaged.

11 Eve - the relief of the 50th Division by 21st Division was
& completed when the 63rd Infantry Brigade took over
12 trenches 67-73 from the 150th Infantry Brigade. The 63rd Infantry Brigade being commanded by Lt Col (temp Brig) HILL. The battalions of this Brigade are 12th West Yorks, 8th Somersets, 8th Lincolns and 10th Yorks and Lancs.

12 10.15pm - town of ARMENTIERES shelled. Presumably the Germans were greeting the arrival of the 21st Division, HQ 21st Division receiving special attention.

14 12th West Yorks were relieved by a regular battalion ie 4th Middlesex Regiment.

 8pm - to commemorate the anniversary of the birth of the Brigade, a gathering assembled at the HQ mess.

16 7.30am - a "strafe" was organised for this date but the weather being unsuitable it was postponed.

17 "Strafe" again postponed on account of the weather. Maj Gen FORESTIER WALKER proceeded to England. Brig Gen G McK FRANKS assumed command of Corps Artillery. Vice Brig Gen A H SHORT Artillery adviser 2 Corps.

18   7.30am - bombardment of FORT SEUARMONT commenced. The Divisional Artillery 21st Division assisted by the 23rd Divisional Artillery took part. In this the "heavies" cooperated with the assistance of aeroplane observation. Considerable damage to the fort was reported.

       10.30am - the enemy retaliated by firing solely into ARMENTIERES and HOUPLINES with "whizz-bangs", French guns (probably taken from LILLE defenses) and 5.9 inch guns. It was noticeable that the damage to houses in the poorer districts was much greater than to those in the better neighbourhoods. The enemy's fire caused the 63rd Infantry Brigade bomb store adjacent to 96th Brigade battle HQ to explode. The bomb store burnt all the afternoon and as it contained Very lights, caused a good pyrotechnic display. Nearly all this Brigades telephonic communications were destroyed by the fire and explosion. It is estimated that the Germans fired between 400 and 500 shell into the town. Total number of rounds fired by this Brigade during the day - 900. We had the last word in the bombardment about 2pm, completely shutting up the enemy's artillery. A certain amount of trouble has been experienced in the Batteries through buffer springs breaking or taking a permanent set and as spares are not carried, guns are out of action much longer than need be necessary.

19   A very quiet day after yesterday's storm Maj Gen CW JACOB C.B. took over command of the Division. Capt JM STEWHOUSE R.A.M.C. joined the Brigade as MO. Vice Lieut PP WARREN transferred to 14th Northumberland Fusiliers.

20-21   Comparatively quiet. Little artillery fire in German side, replied to by double the amount on our side.

22   Quiet.

23   Gen JACOB inspected the gun positions of the Brigade remarking that the men were clean and well set up.

24   Quiet.
25   The enemy shelled with 4.2 Howitzer part of our trenches doing comparatively little damage.
26   We retaliated by the fire of A, B & C Batteries and C/97 (Howitzer Battery), a certain amount of damage was done to their trenches and apparently a bomb store was blown up. The recent issue of two French periscopes to the Brigade has greatly increased the information obtained from observation by our FOOs of the enemy trench line.
27-30 2/Lt LA CONNOLLY slightly wounded (B Battery). Intermittent shelling of town of ARMENTIERES replied to by us with interest.

December 1915; Lieut Colonel RC Coates; ARMENTIERES

1-5   Nothing of importance occurred. The Infantry trenches were much affected by the rain also some of our gun positions, which have to be raised to ground level. Occasional retaliation and counter retaliation.
6   5.30pm - the 459th Howitzer Battery joined the Brigade from the Canadian Division in order to assist in minor operations. The position taken up by the Battery was just south of the ARMENTIERES - LILLE road in the 23rd Division areas (by arrangement with the latter). Battery commander (of 459th Battery) Capt LORD ALFRED BROWNE.
      6pm - two 4.2 shells fell immediately in rear of gun emplacement of B Battery causing the following casualties: 1 OR killed and 4 OR wounded. The latter includes the Battery Sergeant-Major who died whilst being carried to dressing station.
7   B/94 and Capt NANSEN R.G.A. joined this Brigade being attached to this group which is in the right sector

of 21st Division (II Corps), for minor operations and took up position in CHAPELLE D' ARMENTIERES, firing at a range of about 2200 yards to German front line trenches.

8   12 noon - wire cutting 18 pounder Batteries at two points and shelling of CH'AW D'HESPEL and WEZ MACQUART by Howitzer Batteries (C/97 and 459th). Ranges for wire cutting were from 2000 yards - 2500 yards. The results on the wire could not be observed owing to indifferent light.

4pm - D Battery were shelled by a 4.2 Battery and received one direct hit on the top of a gun emplacement. This emplacement was roofed as follows - steel rails laid across a support - two layers of brick rubble in sandbags - one layer of earth in sandbags - on top one layer of brick rubble in sand bags. The shell penetrated the sand bags and cut a steel rail. Thanks to this protection the damage done was comparatively slight to material - the shield and dial sight carrier being bent. Casualties - OR one killed, three wounded.

9   12 noon - the 2nd Army Commander Gen PLUMMER inspected the wagon lines of this Brigade, teams being turned out harnessed up.

2pm-3.30pm - the town of ARMENTIERES was fairly heavily shelled. The wagon lines in PONT DE NIEPPE were also shelled and had to temporarily evacuate their positions. In reply to this the Brigade gave two doses of special retaliation, firing in all some 600 rounds (including about 150 HE). Attached Batteries joined in this retaliation as well. The Army Commander expressed his satisfaction at the condition of the horses and turn out of the harness and wished this to be conveyed to all ranks. At the same time Gen JACOB asked the OC Brigade (Lt Col RC COATES) to express to all ranks that he considered the effect of the shooting on the 8th Dec most satisfactory.

10   9.30-11.30am - enemy shelled the town of ARMENTIERES at intervals.

4.15-4.45pm - enemy shelled the town again, this time heavily. The Brigade HQ (billet) was hit. Casualties - an orderly of B Battery was wounded whilst passing through the town.

11   Brigade HQ moved to another part of town.

12   Very quiet day.

13   The gun positions of the Brigade were inspected by Brig Gen FRANKS, GOCRA II Corps.

14   Quiet.

15   A cutting out expedition having been ordered for the night 15/16, a bombardment was ordered and was undertaken by the artillery of the right sector which consists of 96th Brigade to which is attached C/97, B/94 and 459 Battery (How) (Canadian Division). The object was to destroy enemy's salient and machine guns near point of attack (in conjunction with heavy artillery), to destroy likely machine gun emplacements elsewhere on the line from which fire could brought to bear on the attack, to cut wire at the point of attack and in other places to deceive the enemy. Two Batteries were told off for the actual wire cutting at the point of attack, being given a 25 yard front each. One Battery swept this front and cut narrow lanes about a foot broad at a range of 2000 yards. The other Battery concentrated its fire and cut a lane about a yard broad at a range of 2600 yards. This lane was used by the Infantry in their attack and was reported as excellent. The attack by 120 men of the Somerset LI was timed to take place at 3.15am, night of 15th/16th, the object being to kill and capture Germans and bring back trophies and any information.

It was estimated that it would take 3 minutes for the Infantry to move from our front line to the German parapet. Watches being accurately synchronised, an artillery barrage was begun at 3.18am. This barrage was made about 50 to 100 yards from the furthest point along the trenches that the Infantry were to touch. This barrage was most effective, a complete semi-circle of fire cutting off our own Infantry from any possibility of attack. The Infantry themselves were delighted with our fire and said that they felt absolutely safe within its zone from any enemy attack. The only communication with the attacking party which was received by the 21st Division during the operation, or in fact by the infantry Brigadier in charge, was by means of B Battery (96th) wire to our front line trenches. For the excellent observation resulting on this most successful wire cutting by A Battery, 2/Lt CS KING was awarded a Military Cross. During the day's operations C Battery was shelled and a 4.2 shell landed on top of one of the gun emplacements slightly damaging the gun, killing 3 gunners and wounding the No 1 and two gunners. Congratulatory messages from Army Commander 2nd Army downwards were received.

16   On the conclusion of the above minor enterprise, the 459th Battery was returned to the Canadian Corps and C/96 was sent back to rest for 10 days in Corps Rest Area NOOTE BOOM.

17-18 Quiet. Intermittent shelling.

19   6.45 am - the Germans blew up one mine about 50 yards in front of our front line trenches at the MUSHROOM (I11c. ref map 36 NW).

9am - another mine was blown up alongside the first one by the enemy. When the first mine exploded the SOS signal was given from the trenches. A/96 opened fire in 15 seconds. B/96 and C/97 within a minute. The enemy also fired some 500 rounds onto our support trenches and CHAPELLE d'ARMENTIERES, C/97 coming in for a fair amount of the shell. There were no casualties in the latter Battery except that a wagon was hit. During the night following, B/96 were called on several times to support our bombers in the duel for possession of the craters.

20 Fairly quiet day but at night the Brigade was called upon to repel a German bombing attack on the craters and fire was continued until the O/C Infantry battalion reported that he was satisfied. Congratulations again showered on the Brigade.

21 Fairly quiet during the day. During the night B/96 was called upon to support bombing parties at the craters.

22 Demonstration by the 95th Brigade in which this Brigade assisted.

7.50pm - B and D/96 were called upon to assist the Infantry in repulsing a large bombing party.

23 CHAPELLE d'ARMENTIERES and LILLE ROAD persistently shelled by the enemy.

24 A moderately quiet day, there was a considerable amount of firing on our right and LILLE ROAD was again rather heavily shelled.

Confidential memo from D PAIGE, Capt RFA sent to all units (94th, 95th, 96th Bde RFA), 7.45pm:

The Army Commander has expressed a wish that fire will not be opened up by us on Christmas Day. It is to be clearly understood however that the Germans must not be allowed to take liberties and that, if fire is opened by them, the usual forms of retaliation must be employed. The Army Commander has sent a Christmas Card wishing the Divisional Artillery a Happy Christmas.

25   Having received orders from 2nd Army Commander not to fire except in retaliation, the day was comparatively quiet. The 23rd Division on our right however fired a lot which was evidently the cause of the enemy firing on I1d. (map 36 NW 1/20000) from 11am to noon. Our battle HQ, situated in this square had some narrow escapes.

26   A comparatively quiet day. C/96 returned to its former position in the evening.

27   Bombardment of enemy front line and support trenches opposite MUSHROOM I11c. (Map 36 NW 1/20000) was carried out, the object being to do as much damage as possible to mine shaft. It is probable some damage was done as a quantity of timber and blue clay was seen flying about. The enemy retaliated vigorously especially against A/96. Observers thought this Battery was having a bad time as 50 or 60 4.2 and 5.9 shells fell all round it within a few yards. The only casualties however were two men wounded. These men were carried into a place of safety under heavy shell fire by Sgt DUNSTAN and Gunner WILSON. One gun emplacement was hit and started burning. As the enemy fire was so severe the ammunition wagon in the emplacement could not be withdrawn. Consequently it caught fire and most of the cartridges exploded singly at short intervals. It is worthy of note that no simultaneous explosion of the whole of the ammunition in the wagon took place.

28-29 Quiet.

30   Also quiet. One section of B/96 moved into a position selected to enfilade communication trenches in 23rd Division area (at salient RUE du BOIS (I21b.6½.2½. map 36 NW1/20000) and one section of D/96 moved up to position vacated by A/96 to be able to bombard enemy front parapet at I16d.½.3. These movements were

made in order to cooperate with the 223rd Division in their minor enterprise against I26c.8.4 (enemy salient).

31 Registration was carried out by above sections. C/96 was also called upon to assist in this enterprise. Midnight - we wish the reader of this Diary a more pleasant ending to the coming year, although he may be more favourably situated than we are at present.

Chapter 5
1916 - The Somme

The Winter and Spring of 1916

Jack and the 96th Brigade stayed in the Armentières area until the end of March 1916. During this time there was no major offensive in the British sector of the Western Front; the main fighting at this time was in the area around Verdun in eastern France where the Germans launched an attack against the French on 21st February. This was to be the most important battle of the Great War for France and it lasted until December 1916. It is hard to be certain about casualty figures but a combined total of over 714,200 French and German casualties, of which 262,300 were dead or missing, has been suggested.[1]

Life for Jack during these months was still dangerous; even when there was no big offensive taking place, shellfire was a regular event as each side tried to damage trenches, destroy guns and wear down the morale of their enemy. For example, on the morning of 19th January Jack's battery was attacked:

9.30am - the enemy started shelling on C/96 and continued throughout the day until 4.30pm with an interval of an hour (presumably for lunch) in the middle of the day. ... Altogether about 30 21cm, 80 15cm and 150 10.5cm shell as well as innumerable 7.7cm shell were fired. There were no casualties to personnel but three guns were damaged.[2]

The British artillery was equally busy attacking German lines. As Jack put it:

We have had a rough time of it lately. We have been working night and day for this last month, and very little sleep.[3]

Just how busy they were is indicated by the fact that on 7th February the 21st Division received its ammunition for the week, which consisted of 2000 rounds for the 18 pounder guns and 650 rounds for the 4.5 Howitzer guns.[4]

Occasionally the brigade experienced new events such as on 17th January when it worked in cooperation with an aeroplane for the first time in the war; the aircraft was taking part in observation for the artillery commanders, work which would continue throughout the war.

The weather that winter was variable and the following weather reports were mentioned in the 21st Division War Diary:

> *1st February*   *- very foggy.*
> *5th February*   *- beautifully fine.*
> *22nd February*   *- Weather cold; snow on ground.*
> *25th February*   *- Snow and hard frost.*
> *8th March*   *- Snow fell during the night; beautifully*
>   *fine day.[5]*

Such weather would be no problem for Jack who, as we have seen, was used to the extremes of weather in Bilsdale.

Jack would, by now, be getting used to the routine of life on the front line. One of the highlights of the day would have been meal times. The troops would either be issued with cold rations to cook for themselves or be provided with hot food prepared behind the lines in horse-drawn wheeled cookers. Front-line troops were expected to receive 4,193 calories a day which was less than the Americans' ration of 4,714 calories, when they joined the war in 1918, but slightly more than the Germans' 4,038 calories.[6]

These calories were supposed to consist of 1.25 pounds of fresh meat, 1.25 pounds of bread, 3 ounces of cheese, 4 ounces of bacon, 5/8 ounce of tea, 1/2 ounce of salt, 4 ounces of jam, 3 ounces of sugar and either 8 ounces fresh or 2 ounces dried vegetables[7], but inevitably the reality often fell short of the expectation. The division's Senior Supply Officer regularly wrote in his diary about the failure to acquire the full ration:

22nd January	- *About 50% only of fresh meat on train.*
23rd January	- *6000lbs (33%) of fresh meat only for Division.*
25th January	- *75% of fresh meat and bread.*
5th February	- *Shortage of butter ration. Bacon received in lieu.*
9th March	- *Fresh meat and bread 60%.*
9th April	- *Fresh meat 55%. Preserved meat 45%. Bread 75%.*[8]

The men were also issued with iron rations, consisting primarily of preserved meat and hard dry biscuits, to be used in emergency situations. These were carried by the soldiers at all times and were occasionally eaten in place of normal rations and replaced with new supplies; this was the case for the 21st Division in the middle of April 1916. The diet also changed occasionally when something different appeared on the menu, such as on 22nd February when pea soup was provided.[9]

As well as the army cooks, Jack would also come into contact with vets. The 33rd Mobile Veterinary Section was attached to the 21st Division and regular visits were made to infantry and artillery brigades to check on the horses. In a battle situation the vets were called on to deal with wounded animals but even in quiet times diseases such as tetanus, mange and ringworm had to be treated.[10]

Jack's letters in the spring of 1916 are full of requests for items to be sent; he asks for Oxo cubes, buttons and socks and is also delighted to receive items such as cake, coal tar soap, writing paper and a small stove. Despite living in terrible conditions, he is always concerned about the welfare of friends and family back home; brothers Bob and Ed were both ill that year.

During the last week in March, Jack's battery moved to a rest area and on their return they were ordered to leave Armentières. They travelled around 65 miles by train to Longueau near Amiens and later marched to billets and then to the front line in the area around Meaulte near Albert about 17 miles away. There they took part in daily firing as described above. However this was the calm before the storm; the troops were also starting preparations for the Battle of the Somme which was only a few months away. During this time the command of Jack's battery was changing. For part of May they were temporarily put under the tactical command of the 94th Brigade and then on 15th May there was a reorganisation of the artillery brigades serving with the 21st Division and C Battery, 96th Brigade became C Battery, 97th Brigade. Jack did not have to move areas but the change would have resulted in a change in commanding officer.

Preparations for the Battle of the Somme, April – June 1916

At the Chantilly Conference in November 1915, the Allies had decided to launch a joint offensive on the Western Front during 1916. In the event, the French were not able to participate fully due to their defence of Verdun and it was the British New Army Divisions which were to bear the brunt of the fighting. The timing of the assault was in part chosen in an attempt to relieve pressure on the French by diverting some of the German troops away from Verdun.

Preparations for the offensive were meticulous. General Douglas Haig was in command of the offensive and an important part of his tactics was to have a massive artillery bombardment before the offensive was launched. This, it was believed, would cut enemy barbed wire and destroy trenches and dug-outs meaning that the infantry could simply walk across No Man's Land, capture the destroyed German front-line and launch further attacks from there. Unfortunately it was not quite as simple as that.

In a document entitled _Summary of Preparations for Offensive_, part of the War Diary of the 21st Division for June 1916, the Commanding Officer highlighted some of the difficulties Jack and his colleagues in the Royal Field Artillery - responsible for ensuring the bombardment could take place as Haig planned - had faced.

In early April, on arriving in the area, the division was told to prepare positions for the guns by 27th April. Difficulties soon became apparent such as the fact that the area being prepared was over-looked by land in German occupation, the lack of Royal Engineer support and the lack of time allowed - the 27th April deadline was later brought forward by one week.

There were also other problems:

> _It was impossible to obtain steel shelters for gun emplacements, pit props and, at times even sandbags were not forthcoming._
>
> _The scarcity of wire and the promise that none would be available made it very necessary to cut down communications to absolute essentials. Finally it transpired that wire could have been available so we suffered from want of really knowing what would be available._
>
> _Work progressed slowly because:_
> _• lack of personnel, Battery wagon lines being far distant from the scene of action and the inability to obtain more than a few infantry._
> _• most of the work could only be undertaken at night._
> _• Batteries building positions were also in action and had to keep some men at the guns._

There were also problems with the supply of ammunition. Each 18 pounder gun was supposed to have 1000 rounds and each 4.5 Howitzer, 800 rounds, which had to be dumped at the guns prior to the start of operations. The division was given 18 days to form dumps, and ammunition was brought to three forward railheads and delivered to battery positions by motor lorry. In the end, all the ammunition was dumped on time but difficulties arose because the principal railhead was some miles out of the divisional area. Unloading and delivering had to take place at night at a time when nights were at their shortest and ammunition trains frequently arrived late, often with a different load from the one expected. This lack of control and organisation in divisional arrangements made things unnecessarily difficult for men on the ground.

18-pounder battery in action in the open (IWM Q.2017)

It is clear reading this diary that the Commander was somewhat surprised that his units were more or less ready when the day arrived. He wrote:

More "cunning" might have been used in compiling the scheme in small details had more time been available. As is bound to be the case there were many changes and alterations but all was ready when the flag fell at 4.30am on 24th June.[11]

The Senior Supply Officer was also busy during these preparations. Extra iron rations for the troops were issued or placed in supply dumps and gun positions and iron rations for horses were also issued.[12]

The bombardment started on 24th June and was due to last five days until 28th June when the attack was planned. In the event the offensive was postponed for 48 hours due to bad weather (it rained heavily from 26th–28th June) and the bombardment lasted a further two days. In total during the week, 1,437 guns fired 1,508,652 shells at a cost of approximately £6 million.[13]

The impact of this bombardment on the enemy can be seen in the following account:

From nine till ten, the shelling acquired a demented fury. The earth shook, the sky seemed like a boiling cauldron. Hundreds of heavy batteries were crashing away at and around Combles, innumerable shells criss-crossed hissing and howling over our heads. All was swathed in thick smoke, which was in the ominous underlighting of coloured flares. Because of racking pains in our heads and ears, communication was possible only by odd, shouted words. The ability to think logically and the feeling of gravity, both seemed to have been removed.[14]

Each battery was given specific targets for their shooting and men were told to be ready to fire gas shells if the wind was in the right direction. However what the British did not know was that German trenches and dug-outs were much better fortified than British ones. One must add to this the fact that many of the shells were defective - either they did not explode at all or they were not powerful enough to destroy the German defences. Haig's plan, which had seemed perfect, was not working and the Commander of the 21st Division wrote at the end of June:

> *long range observation makes the cutting of wire a matter of uncertainty.*[15]

It was soon to become clear that the Commander's opinion was correct; despite the long bombardment, the wire had not been destroyed.

The Battle of the Somme, July - November 1916

As will be clear from the above, when the whistles blew at 7.30am on 1st July and infantry regiments along the front line climbed out of their trenches, instead of facing no resistance, they found the Germans ready and waiting. Machine guns literally mowed down men as they moved across the open ground and, at the end of the first day, 19,240 men were dead, 35,493 were wounded, 2,152 were missing and 585 had been taken prisoner. This gives a total of 57,470 casualties.[16] The average expenditure of ammunition per gun of the 21st Division on 1st July was 368 rounds and this constant firing of shells must have been too much for many men.[17] On 30th June the 21st Division had consisted of 21,387 men and 5,420 animals. On 3rd July the Senior Supply Officer drew rations for only 15,983 men and 5,377 horses. He notes that the division was congratulated by the Army Commander on its successes and splendid work but quickly goes on to note that the estimated number of casualties is 6,500.[18]

In the days that followed some small gains were made. The 21st Division was attacking in the area around Fricourt and this village was captured on 2nd July. Over the following days the artillery brigades continued to fire in support of infantry attacks and the division advanced a few miles. This was at a heavy cost and the casualty rate continued to be high for both men and animals - in July 1916, 206 injured horses were evacuated from the 21st Division, often due to shrapnel wounds.[19]

Empty 18-pounder shell cases after the bombardment of Fricourt, July 1916 (IWM Q.113)

The 21st Division was still having problems with faulty equipment and on 4th July the diary notes:

Trouble with springs [for guns] *continues. No-one possesses springs and they cannot be obtained from the base.*[20]

The attack continued throughout July. Unfortunately the 97th Brigade's diary for this month was destroyed by shellfire so we cannot be sure which actions Jack took part in or whether he had any rest. Around 1st August however, the 21st Division was ordered to relieve the 14th Division near Arras, and the 97th Brigade marched to the north. No information is given about the route taken by Jack, but the 94th Brigade's diary records that its men marched for 75 miles to reach the same destination. Jack's battery was soon bombarding enemy trenches although at least the men were now out of the area of the main battle zone.

At the end of August the artillery of the 21st Division was again reorganised. C Battery, 97th Brigade became C Battery, 94th Brigade. Once again Jack had a new commanding officer.

On 8th September new orders were received and, soon after, the 94th Brigade marched 38 miles (using a much more direct route) back to the area they had left in July. For the next month they continued to be part of the main Battle of the Somme attacks and casualties were heavy; 43 men were killed or wounded from 14th - 28th September and 48 from 1st - 14th October.

In an attempt to strengthen the attack, the British turned to a new and untested weapon – the tank. These were first used in combat on 15th September 1916 near Delville Wood. The 94th Brigade was in that area and it is possible that Jack witnessed this event. In the Brigade's diary, Colonel Banister wrote

> *"Tanks" first employed on this day - proved to be a success.*[21]

On 14th October Jack left the fighting on the Somme and with his brigade marched 75 miles over 6 days to Lapugnoy west of Béthune to the north of Arras. In late October they took up positions but Jack was not involved in a bombardment until 7th November.

It seems that with the changes of brigade and location, post may have become somewhat irregular in September and October 1916. On 25th October Jack wrote to his parents:

> *I now take pleasure in answering your ever welcome letter and parcel I recieved this morning. I can't explain how delighted I was to hear from you again, and all of you were keeping in the best of health. Mrs Stephenson sent me a*

parcel on Sept. 10th which I have never recieved yet, and won't now. I expect it is through changing our Address, you see I could only let you know that I had changed my Address, and after that we could not get letters away at all. Oh just come in one letter from you one letter from Bob and three papers from Mrs Stephenson all addressed 97 Bde and posted in September.[22]

In his letters Jack often mentions other men from Bilsdale serving in the army but despite none of his brothers joining up, he is not very sympathetic to those who are not doing their duty:

I am pleased old Loll Dale has to send two of his sons to join up. They haven't half showed them up for being shirkers.[23]

The Battle of the Somme finally ended in mid November when the weather got too bad to continue attacking. Away from the Somme area Jack's brigade continued bombarding the enemy until the end of the year. Although the number of casualties decreased there was still no rest from the war. Two Christmases on from the optimistic days of August 1914, the Great War was still a long way from its end.

Letters 1916

1. Field Postcard from Jack to Gladys [January 5th 1916]

I am quite well
I have received your letter dated 25th 15
I have received your parcel dated 25th 15
Letter follows at first opportunity
     J. W. Garbutt

2. Letter from Jack to Mary Emma and Isaac [January 6th 1916]

Dear Mother and Father

just a few lines in answer to your last letter which I recieved the other day. I was pleased to hear that you all were getting on well and had a nice Christmas. Well Xmas passed like any other day out here we never new it was Xmas. I received Gladys's parcel. We were at a rest camp when it came and I was pleased to have a cake sent from Mother. We were only they 10 days and we new it. I should have sooner have been in action 20 times over. We were up to the knees in nothing else but mud. I haven't had any parcel from Mrs Bennison yet. We have had a few lively times with the Germans out here. We let them know when New Year came. Oh it was just like a flame in the trenches. I had three nice cards from cousin Bob and a letter. I had a parcel sent from Mrs Stephenson. Well it will be to late when you recieve this letter to send anything in the parcel you are gong to send me. Their is not anything particular I want oxo cubes come in very handy when I am on sentry pair of socks would come in handy for I am never done having wet feet. Oh and send some of those Bathelors buttons for I cant keep a button on my breeches. My mate that used to billet with me at

Berkhamsted as got killed in action out here. Well I think that is all I can mention this time hoping these few lines will find you all well as it leaves me in the best of spirits from Your loving Son

      J.W. Garbutt xx
         Good bye

Addrress Gnr_____ 63978
C Batty 96 Bde
R.F.A. B.E. Force

3. Post Card/Birthday Card from Gladys to Jack [January 1916]

To dear Jack with best wishes for a Happy Birthday & Many more to come with best love from your ever Loving sister Gladys.

Thanks very much for the pretty Christmas Card. Haven't heard a word about your parcel yet I sent you on Dec *[illegible]*.

4. Letter from Mary Emma to Jack [January 18th 1916]

My dearest Jack

I was delighted when I got your last letter saying you had got the parcel alright, I hope you have sent Mrs B__ a word of thanks I told her you had got her parcel alright & she says she is going to get the girls to knit you some socks before long I thought it was very kind of her indeed. Well dear Jack it was a trial to me when I knew feet were always wet. I am sending you some socks soon and some Oxo cubes & Batchelors Buttons for you so you must book out before long for them I would have sent them before if you had let me know. I was sorry you could not spend a better Xmas but live in hopes for something better after a while there will be plenty of men in another few weeks they all have to go that can be spared they are starring all the best farmers. that means that they are only left a little longer. what Bob has got done about I dont know for we have not heard a work since Xmas Willie Metcalfe goes on Thursday he would like to get in the R.F.A. but it is closed now. they have been given every chance so they have only theirselves to blame poor old Geo Garbutt is buried to day at Seave Green. there is a lot of lads from about here in France so might easily come accross some one you know well dear Jack I think I have told you all. Poor Ed has gone to the hospital but he has not been operated upon yet I will write & let you know how he is going on I am sending you Gladys & my photo we got them taken solely that you could have one so with all our love and kisses to you my dear one & hopes that the Lord will watch over you & keep you safe from all harm Believe me

Always Your Loving Mother

M. E. Garbutt

5. Letter from Jack to Mary Emma and Isaac [Monday 31st 1916 - probably January]

Dear Mother and Father

I have found time at last to write a few lines. We have had a rough time of it lately. We have been working night and day for this last month, and very little sleep. I will tell you all about it if I ever come home. Sergant Jones has won the D.C.M. he is in our Battery. We never had a man killed or wounded, but we can thank the captain for that Well I am still in good health and best of spirits and I hope these few lines to find you all the same. I received your parcel last night and I was pleased with the socks and the small things that were in the box. I was in need of a pair of socks badly till I got those two new pair, and now I am well set up. I hope you will thank Miss Parry and Mrs

Atkinson for their kindness, and I thank you very much for the parcel the cake went down extra. I had a parcel sent from Mrs Stephenson the other day, a cake and a little stove. They the handiest thing a man could carry about with him out here you can heat any thing up when you like. It is very kind of her I am sure that is the second parcel from her. She said she had heard it was my birthday in January but she had forgot the Date. I have never heard from bob for a long time now. Well I hope poor old Ed pulls through his operation alright and goes on well and that he may be alright ever after. Well I think I have told you all this time I dare write, well with best wishes and kisses from your Loving Son

    J.W. Garbutt

      xxxxx

Good Night and cheer up

This is Jacks last letter *[written in a different hand, probably Mary Emma's]*

6. Letter from Jack to Gladys [February 3rd 1916]

Dear Gladys

    just a few lines to let you know that I am not dead yet. You will think me a long time in writing but I really have not had time. You will perhaps want to know why but I can't tell you in a letter. Well I hope their is kno harm done for it is old Fritz's fault. I got the card and parcel you sent me all were safe and sound. The soap came in very handy at the time for I had not a bit. The coal tar soap was the best for you could both wash and shave with it. I got the photo of mother and you, and I think they are quite natural, you both have taken well. I believe I forgot to put in Mothers letter that I had got the card but you can tell them just as well. Tell Mother the writing paper was very useful and send some more next time. I was in a hurry when I wrote her letter and I didn't put half in that I intended to do. I will bring you that ring home if God spares me too. Miss Parry's socks fit a treat and are just think thing for wear and warmth. Well Gladys thank her for her kindness and that I said so. I had a nice parcel from Mrs Stephenson for my birthday. Well I think that is all this time Gladys, hoping these few lines will find you in the best of health as it leaves me in the pink so with best wishes and kisses from your loving Brother

> J. W. Garbutt
> > Ta Ta
> > > Bon Soir

7. Postcard sent from Mrs A M Stephenson to Jack [April 15th 1916]

192 Coltman St, Hull
Ap. 15. 1916

I have been looking for a line from you for some weeks now and if you are in Hospital I should be so glad if anyone wld send me word, that yr Parents & I can communicate. Now if you are only "very busy" please drop me a p.c. to say if you can do with a refill for yr cooker & I will send it along with a cake. My son is in the same part as you are now. I shall look for a word everyday.

> Mrs A M Stephenson

8. Field Postcard from Jack to Gladys [May 8th 1916]

I am quite well
I have received your letter dated 7/5/16
Letter follows at first opportunity
> J. W. Garbutt

9. Letter from Jack to Mary Emma and Isaac [7th 16??]

Dear Mother and Father

just a few lines in answer of your ever welcome letter. You will think me a long time in dropping a few lines, but time as been scarce. I am still in good health and spirits I heard Bob had been very bad with phneomonia and plurosy. I was pleased to hear he had a good home and every care could be taken of him. He wants to take care of himself when he gets out. Well I hope he will soon be better. I have been Inoculated again and got over it alright. We are having jolly fine weather out here now. I recieved the parcel from Gladys safe and sound, and what a treat to taste a bit of Mothers home made cake. Well I haven't got much to say this time as things are pretty quiet at present. I think the Germans having taken on a costly job at Verdun, I don't think that they will ever see Verdun now. Well I think that is all this time hoping these few lines will find you all in the best of health from your ever loving Son

      J.W. Garbutt

        xxxxxxx

            Good Night and God bless till we meet again

10. Extract from a letter from Mrs A M Stephenson to Mary Emma [22nd May 1916]

Bethrapha
Glossop
Derbyshire

Dear Mrs Garbutt, my dear friend

....I had another nice letter from Jack on the 14th in the last parcel I had sent him a book & he was so pleased that I posted off another one the other day. he says they are in a lonely place just now and it is nice he can enjoy a good read. When we returned from Harrogate we were grieved to hear that Elmer in his first experience of the trenches has been exposed to so much rain & liquid mud that when they were relieved they found he was stiff with rheumatism, had to be lifted and then conveyed in a cart & on an officer's horse which his lieutenant kindly got for him but thank God the attack passed off in two days & he never intended us to know at all but the news came through others. He writes very cheerfully from "my little grey hut in the Avenue" & says he slept through a heavy bombardment one night, only rousing to cover his face as bits of earth were dropping onto it. Dear lads, are they not brave. Yes I can imagine how pretty Bilsdale is; the scenery here is most charming, we have some beautiful walks in many directions we are 1500ft above sea level, hills surround us on every side I am pleased you were able to go to the early service at Easter & can picture how your heart would rise in thanksgiving to Our God and Father. May all our lives be His

> Your loving friend
> A M Stephenson

11. Field Postcard from Jack to Gladys [July 6th 1916]

I am quite well
I have received your letter dated 3/7/16
Letter follows at first opportunity
> J. Garbutt

12. Letter from Jack to Mary Emma and Isaac [August 6th 1916]

My Dear Mother and Father
  I now take the pleasure in writing a few lines, you will think me a long time, but I always write when I get time I recieved

your parcel with the greatest of pleasure. I recieved two parcels and papers from Mrs Stephenson, and I never had time to write her a letter yet. I shall have plenty of time now. I hope you are all keeping well and in the best of health as it leaves me the same. We are having grand weather here. I should think you will have finished hay-time by now. I think Mrs Stephenson and company are coming up to Ingleby for their holidays this summer. I have never seen Ben Cousans yet nor have I heard from him. We are in their quarters now so I am looking out for him. I could not send that photo so I cut it down, and now I can carry it with me. So I will now conclude with my very best wishes and heaps of kisses from your ever loving Son

     J.W. Garbutt xxxxxx

       Bon Soir

13. Letter from Jack to Gladys [August 8th 1916]

My dear Gladys

  just a few lines to show you I haven't forgot you all together. Well to tell the truth I have never had time to write till now. Its seems ages since I heard from you. Well I hope you are keeping well as it leaves me in best of health. We are having glorious weather over here now. Well I wonder what old fritz think to the New Army now he used to laugh at us before we began our offensive. I see in the papers the Zepps have been over England again. Well I think that is all this time, so with best wishes & kisses from your loving Brother

     J.W. Garbutt xxxx

       My best regards to John

14. Letter from Jack to Gladys [Aug 26ᵗʰ 1916]

My Dear Gladys
  just a few lines in answer of your ever welcome letter I recieved a few days ago. I hope you are keeping in the best of health, as it leaves me the same. I know what a busy time you will have when you have to manage visitors by yourself. They take a lot of looking after. I have had a letter from bob, but he dosen't say much about the squabble. I think they are all settled down again, except the poor girl and she as had to leave. She was a good girl too I saw that the first time I so her. I suppose Mother is down at Nottingham this week-end. I hope she as a nice time, and the weather keeps fine for her. I wish I had been they with her it would have been jolly fine wouldn't it. Nottingham is a fine place I suppose. I know a few chaps from there. Well I think that is all this time So now I will conclude withlove and best wishes from your loving brother xxxxxx
  J.W. Garbutt
  Oh how is John getting on my best wishes
  Write Soon won't you
  ta ta

15. Part letter from Jack to Mary Emma and Isaac [October 25ᵗʰ 1916]

My Dear Mother and Father
  I now take pleasure in answering your ever welcome letter and parcel I recieved this morning. I can't explain how delighted I was to hear from you again, and all of you were keeping in the best of health. Mrs Stephenson sent me a parcel on Sept 10th which I have never recieved yet, and won't now. I expect it is through changing our Address, you see I could only let you know that I had changed my Address, and after that we could not get letters away at all. Oh just come in one letter from you

one letter from Bob and three papers from Mrs Stephenson all addressed 97 Bde and posted in September. Mrs Stephenson has sent me her photo, and what a nice old lady she looks dosen't she. I recieved the P.O. Arthur sent me and I thank him very much for his kindness I wish to have a day or two shooting with him if I come out of this lot alright. It was a good barricade Arthur put up for me you could just lean over the top and nip anything off that came within range of you. The old cock pheasants shied at it when they so it, and a good job too. How did Ed come on when he went up....

16. Letter from Jack to Mary Emma and Isaac [November 12th 1916]

My Dear Mother and Father
   just a few lines in answer of your ever welcome letter I recieved safely on the 11th. I recieved the paper too. I am pleased old Loll Dale has to send two of his sons to join up. They haven't half showed them up for being shirkers. I expect bob will have to go at the finish well he has had a good time off. I have seen poor Ben Cousans at last he is only 500 yards away from me. He has got a good job now he is in a soup kitchen. He asked after you all, and said he was going to send you a card. He asked especially about Gladys and if she was still at the Vicarage. He said he had many a bit of sport watching Father chase us with a big stick when we were young at home he said his chief words used to be "Damn ya" and he was right too. I laugh when I think about that. Poor Ben has failed a lot since his poor Mother died. Tears came into his eyes when he talked about her. I am glad Ed has got a good heart for joining the army if they want him. It is best to be voluntary than it is to be dragged their. Mrs Stephenson wants one of my Photos if you have got one to send her. She as asked me for one in return of that one she sent to me Well I said she could have one if she wanted one. I have had

a nice letter from Gladys Well I think that is all to night as (Je suis fatigue) I am tired So now I will conclude hoping these few lines find you all well as it leaves me in the best of health with love and best wishes from Your loving son

J.W. Garbutt

xxxxxxx

Bon Soir

17. Part letter from Jack to Mary Emma and Isaac [probably December 1916 or January 1917]

... a birthday card. But I wish you many happy returns of the day. What do you think to the Kaisers peace proposals, I think he wants it all in his own favour, but that can't be done. If he wants peace he must accept our peace terms. I think he must be feeling the pinch of war now "don't you think so". I must close now, Wishing you all a happy Xmas, and a bright and prosperous New year when it comes with all good wishes from your ever loving Son

J. W. Garbutt

18. Post card of Great Broughton sent from Mrs Foulger to Jack [Date unknown]

Dear Jack

Just a few views of your native home with love from us all

Yours sincerely

Mrs Foulger

Xxx

96th Brigade RFA, War Diary 1916
January 1916; Lt Colonel RC Coates;
ARMENTIERES

1-2   Quiet days.

3   For a considerable time during the middle of the day B/94 Battery was very heavily shelled. No damage however was done to equipment. 4.2 and 5.9 Batteries took part in this shelling. B/94 moved out to their wagon lines the same night.

4-5   Nothing of interest.

6   Enemy bombarded trenches 69, 70 and 71 and bombed the MUSHROOM at I11c.2.5. We retaliated with all Batteries.

7   A Battery returned from rest area at NOOTE BOOM and took up B/96 position at I3c.4.1. B/96 moved out to rest area.

8   As the Germans on their side of the crater have been during the last few days putting up brushwood revetements and making themselves generally disagreeable at this point, it was decided to try and knock down this cover. Trench Mortars (2") were employed together with C/97 (4.5") to carry this out, A/96 (18pdr) being used to keep the enemy's heads down along their parapet. Considerable damage was done to the revetement, the enemy retaliating on the MUSHROOM.

9-10   Quiet days.

11   10am - D/96 was heavily shelled. The enemy fire lasted some three hours, the rate of fire being rapid at first and afterwards slackening off to one round a minute and then to one round every two minutes. The total number of shell fired is estimated at 105 heavy shell including 4.2", 5.9" and 8" and 25 whizz bangs. Among the pieces picked up was the nose of what was apparently an armour piercing projectile. No damage was done to

men or equipment although shell fell all round the guns. 11pm - a minor enterprise having been ordered in the left sector opposite PONT BALLOT (C29c.4½.9½), a bombardment and wire cutting was ordered for this hour and timed for 11.15pm, ie 20 minutes before the moon set. This Brigade stood by for retaliation and counter Battery work but our assistance was not required.

12 Quiet day.

13 Some 40 rounds of 80mm ammunition were fired into CHAPELLE D'ARMENTIERES otherwise everything was quiet in our sector.

14 Again the only event of interest was the 80mm gun on CHAPELLE D'ARMENTIERES. This gun seems to be very harmless in its effect.

15 In the morning a 15cm Howitzer put 16 rounds into D Battery. Eight of these were blind and no damage was done. A Battery fired on a small bridge, screened by a brown canvas screen. One of the rounds hit a dugout nearly causing an explosion (I11c.6.7). 7.50pm - the enemy put some 20 rounds into the town a later put one or two rounds in every half hour until about 1am. The 2nd Army Heavy group retaliated on LILLE but this Brigade did not fire. In the Gazette of 1.1.16 the following officers and men of this Brigade were "mentioned in dispatches" Lt Col RC COATES D.S.O., Major T McGOWAN, Lieut SD TIMSON, Lieut CS KING Corp RWJ COOK, Gnr T TAYLOR. In the London Gazette of 13.1.16 the following honours were published Companion of the D.S.O. Maj T McGOWAN (D).

16 Nothing of interest.

17 8.30am - we cooperated with an aeroplane for the first time in this war.
11.30am - one of our aeroplanes, which was flying very low for special observations was heavily fired on by hostile Infantry. Three of our Batteries opened fire and succeeded

in stopping most of the fire of rifles and machine guns. 7.40pm - the enemy put about 30 shell into the town but the remainder of the night was quiet.

18 No event of interest.

19 9.30am - the enemy started shelling on C/96 and continued throughout the day until 4.30pm with an interval of an hour (presumably for lunch) in the middle of the day. A hostile aeroplane ranged the enemy Batteries at the start of the shoot and again early in the afternoon. Altogether about 30 21cm, 80 15cm and 150 10.5cm shell as well as innumerable 7.7cm shell were fired. There were no casualties to personnel but three guns were damaged as follows: one gun dismounted and practically destroyed, two guns outer spring cases altogether broken up. There were no direct hits on the guns. The emplacements were made of semicircular iron cylinders with three layers of sandbags all over. These were very badly knocked about. I consider that if they are placed on top of the ground that they are inclined to be top heavy. They must however in these cases be so placed, as the gun emplacements fill with water when made below the surface of the ground. Orders were issued to the batteries not to go to their gun positions under cover of darkness (they had previously been withdrawn) as we have found that it is the usual custom of the enemy to drop occasional rounds on a battery position at night when that position has been heavily shelled during the day in order to catch any men who may be working at the débris. When the shelling first started this morning, Sgt A JONES with great bravery under heavy shell fire went to each gun emplacement, these being widely scattered, and removed and brought in all the dial sights, making two journeys to do this, He did this because he knew that on former occasions, even with limited hostile shelling, these sights were generally broken.

20   C Battery removed their damaged guns and withdrew to their wagon line, pending the preparation of a new position.

21-22 Nothing of interest.

23   Nothing of interest. D/96 enfiladed PRMESQUES ROAD (I17 and I24) at intervals during the day - some 10 rounds being fired. This is done most days as the road is used by the enemy.

24   B/96 (one section) cut the wire in front of the southern sap out to the mine craters. One gun was shooting rather erratically and the O/C B Battery unfortunately did not confine the shooting to the other gun which was shooting well, so that a certain number of rounds were wasted. The Infantry expressed themselves as satisfied with the lane cut which was about 4 yards wide. The knife-rests, which were of iron, were knocked down flat, the supports were broken by the shells. About 200 Shrapnel and 50 HE were used. This number includes rounds used to cut another lane in the wire opposite the northern sap out to the mine crater (as a blind to the enemy).

25   9.55pm - 21st Divisional Cyclists made an attempt to enter the German southern sap (to the craters) which is not more than 20 yards from our sap on the near side of the craters. They, however, found the Germans ready (with a strong bombing party in the sap) and they withdrew from the unequal contest.

26   Heavy shelling of infantry trenches on both sides. Afternoon quiet.

27   Kaiser's birthday. We thought great things would happen. Nothing much happened on our immediate front. A few hundred shells were dropped all over the place but did practically no damage. Some 50 rounds fell round D/96 Battery's positions but beyond wounding one man (by the first shell) no damage was done.

11.15pm - the Division on our right was heavily shelled

and asked for assistance which was given by A/96.

28 Orders were received to make a change in the telephones by removing the connection between the "L ou E terminal" and the base plate and also to lay the line back to the earth pin (from the front trenches) along the same course and as parallel to the outward line. This was rendered necessary on account of reports being received that the enemy could still hear our telephone messages.

31 C/96 moving into their new position which they had been preparing during the preceding days. Cooperation was asked for by the 23rd Division to assist in a cutting out expedition. The Germans however spotted it in its initial stage and having waited for 4 hours we received orders that the expedition was off.

February 1916; Lt Colonel R C Coates; ARMENTIERES; Sheet 36 NW 1/20000

1-4 No event of importance.

5 A kite balloon observed fire from B13a.4.8 on a gun position I24c.2.6. The results were not very satisfactory as regards either range or line, as "OK" was given at about 300 yards over and to the left of the target.

5+6 A new system of holding the trenches was adopted in the Division. The Divisional front was divided into 2 sectors instead of 3 and front line trenches in each sector were held by 2 battalions. In consequence of this A/94 and C/94 covering the left of the Right sector were put under orders of the OC 96th Brigade in the event of urgent calls. This necessitated certain changes in the position of dugouts and FOOs.

7-11 No unusual activity during this period on either side.

12 2.05pm - very violent bombardment by the enemy of trenches in the Right sector and many points in rear. The

enemy appeared to be trying to cut our wire and it was much damaged by their fire. The FOO of B/96, thinking the enemy were about to attack, gave the SOS call. This intense bombardment lasted about 20 minutes.

9.15pm - the enemy again bombarded our front line trenches for a short time.

13 Our trenches were bombarded steadily the whole day. Trench 68 was heavily shelled with field guns, field howitzers and 15cm howitzers. A shell fell into the officers mess of A/96 but luckily it did not explode and there were no casualties. All suspected gun positions, also front line trenches, were shelled by us. The area in rear of our trenches was also heavily shelled by the enemy.

14 Quiet day.

15 Quiet day in Right sector. The batteries of this Brigade were held in readiness for counter battery work in connection with an organised bombardment by the Artillery of the Left sector of the enemy's lines in the neighbourhood of PONT BALLOT salient.

16 Nothing of interest.

17 A shoot was carried out against certain selected spots in the enemy's front line and in rear of it, resulting in no activity on the part of the enemy. It is reported that the Saxons have relieved the Wurtemburgers in our part of the line (by one of our FOOs).

18 11.30pm - operations were carried out against front line and communications trenches near L'EPINETTE. Batteries of 96th Brigade RFA were ordered to be ready for counter battery work.

19 The Brigade stood by for counter battery work, the Division being ordered to bomb L'EPINETTE. We were not called upon to open fire.

20 The enemy however retaliated on our trenches to the north.

21 During the whole day, with short interval for lunch, 4.2s

and possibly guns of a larger calibre were mis-directed against D/96 and therefore did no damage.

22　Nothing of interest.

23　C/97 and A/96 had a small combined shoot against a house which was supposed to contain a gun.

24　Minor operation against enemy's trenches. Wire was cut for a distance of 20 yards at I11a.4.3. Allotment of ammunition - 120 Shrapnel, 40 HE. The HE was reported to be quite useless for this as with the "No 2 gaine" they ricocheted off the hard ground and burst in the air. Orders were received for a bombardment of the enemy's front line trenches from 10.57pm-11.30pm. Our infantry were ordered to assault at 11pm onto the trenches at I5c.7.1 to I5c.8.3. At 11pm also, D/96, which was covering this part of the enemy's trenches were ordered to gradually lift their fire. At 11.15pm the order to stop fire was however given and we subsequently heard that the reason was that the infantry had failed to enter the German trenches.

25　Gen Sir FERGUSON, (the II Corps Commander) inspected the Battery positions. Orders have been received that we shall be relieved between the 1st and 10th March.

26-29　Nothing of special interest.

March 1916; Lt Colonel RC Coates; ARMENTIERES; Sheet 36 NW 1/20000

1-2　Nothing to report.

3　Right sector carried out bombardment of the enemy's trenches opposite the MUSHROOM, I11c.3.4 with the object of destroying the enemy's works. 300 rounds were fired from B/96 and the same from C/96. Fire commenced by 1.30pm and was finished by 2.40pm. C/97 (Howitzers) also took part as well as Trench

Mortars. Large gaps were made and the parapet was badly damaged. Many 18 pounder no 100 fuze and no 2 gaine burst on ricochet.

4   5pm - the enemy put 50 rounds into ARMENTIERES. We retaliated against enemy front line trenches - 40 rounds per Battery. The remaining artillery of the Division also retaliated.

5-9   Nothing of interest. There were a good many snowstorms during these days. A certain amount of counter battery work was done, also shelling of spots where in fine weather working parties had been observed. Calico was purchased and placed on the ground underneath the muzzles of guns to conceal the bare patches made in the snow by the blast of the guns.

10-13   No event of importance.

14   Trench Mortars fired on the railway salient I11a.4.2. This drew a certain amount of retaliation onto trenches 72 and 73 and necessitated counter battery work from the Brigade.

15   C/97 had been for some days quietly shooting at PERENCHIES church, an important enemy OP. Large pieces have been taken out of the church and tower - the latter having now a considerable list to the south.

16   Counter battery work. Orders were issued as to our relief by the 80th Brigade (Col CARDEW) of the 17th Division. Battery commanders of the relieving Brigade came over to view the position. Batteries have been ordered to move direct to rest area near LA KREULE (B16b.9.8, sheet 27 1/40000) on the following dates: March 18th - 1 section A/96 and B/96, 19th - A/96 and B/96 less 1 section each, 21st - Ammunition Column, 22nd - 1 section C/96 and D/96, 23rd - C/96 and D/96 less one section each and Brigade HQ. During the winter months up to date we have had 12 successful shoots with

aeroplane observation. Owing to reports being received of messages being overheard by the enemy, a complete system of metallic telephone circuits has been installed between batteries and battalion commanders, company commanders and FOOs, also all station calls have been changed in accordance with *II Corps G77 (34/2)* dates 1.3.16.

17   10.30am - the orderly officer 80th Brigade RFA arrived to take over Brigade HQ. He left again at 1.30pm. 2/Lt CRD SCHAGEL (B) who was wounded on 27.2.16 was struck off the strength having been invalided to England.

18   1 section of A and B moved to rest area east of HAZEBROUCK. On handing over the wires for communications for 4 Batteries from Divisional Artillery HQ, through 96th Brigade HQ, through battle area HQ, thence to Batteries HQ and FOOs it was estimated that 16 miles of wire of all natures was in use and 25 miles more laid and under Battery arrangements.

20   A & B less 1 section moved to rest area as above.

21   Ammunition column moved to rest area.

22   1 section C and D moved to rest.

23   C & D less 1 section and Brigade HQ moved to rest area. Lt RL NASH left to takeover duties of Adjutant of 97th Brigade RFA.

24-29   Rest. During this period GOC 2nd Army inspected B/96 and expressed himself as highly satisfied by the work done by the Brigade during the period it was part of the 2nd Army at ARMENTIERES.

30   LA KREULE. Advance party under Capt MELLE proceeded to new area. 4th Army XIII corps at BUSSY near AMIENS.

31   HQ 96th Brigade A Battery and ¼ Ammunition Column moved to new area by train, the journey taking about 9 hours, and detrained at LONGUEAU.

April 1916; Maj F H Courtney; BUSSY les DAOURS

1	B C D Batteries and rest of Ammunition Column (less ¼ moved to new area. Detrained at LONGUEAU.
2-4	Rest.
5	Brigade Commander and Orderly Officer reconnoitred Battery positions east of MEAULTE. Lt Col COATES ordered to England to command the artillery of a Division.
7	Lt COATES left for England. Maj COURTNEY temporarily in command of the Brigade.
9	Working parties from A and B Batteries proceeded to the front to construct battery positions.
11	1 section of C/96 went into action in positions east of MEAULTE. 1 OR B/96 wounded.
12	1 OR A/96 wounded.
15	Working parties from C and D Batteries proceeded to the front to construct battery positions. 1 OR C/96 wounded.
16	Maj COURTNEY appointed to the command of the Brigade.
23	A and B Battery positions under construction heavily shelled, no casualties.
26	Lt RB WITHERS to 21st Heavy Siege Battery.

May 1916; Lt Colonel Courtney; BUSSY les DAOURS

1-4	Nothing to report.
4	10.30pm - orders were received to move A & B Batteries into action in the positions they were building in F1c. (sheet 62D NE) on the 5th inst. D Battery and the remaining section of C Battery were to move up the following evening. As positions for C and D Batteries were not ready for occupation, the section of C Battery

was ordered to occupy emplacements near A/94, at BELLEVUE FARM and became tactically the third section of A/94. D Battery were ordered to occupy 4 out of the 12 French emplacements in F19b. The object of the move was merely for defensive purposes only, in order to have one gun per 75 yards of line. These Batteries were placed tactically in the 94th Brigade group (Col BANNISTER) but remained for administrative purposes under the OC 96th Brigade.

5 BECORDEL 9.30pm - A and B Batteries brought up the guns. While A Battery was getting their guns into the emplacements the enemy put over about 30 4.2" and 5.9" shell in and around the position. No damage was done, the drivers and the teams behaving splendidly inspite of the fact that one 5.9 shell fell between two teams.

6 C and D Batteries moved up into action. Brigade Ammunition Column moved up to BUIRE. Brigade HQ were temporarily established in Redoubt 19 in E12b.

7 A and B Batteries registered a few points in the enemy's lines. The enemy retaliated with a few rounds but no damage was done.

8 C and D Batteries registered a few points. The Right section of C Battery (BELLEVUE FARM) was given a portion of the line to cover, but A, B and D Batteries were ordered not to fire except in the case of a general attack, and the minimum amount of registration to be done.

9-15 A and B Batteries were kept busy improving their present positions and C and D continued to build their new positions while in action in the positions they went into on 6th. Orders had been received that all guns and ammunition pits, telephone huts etc should have burster roofs and a second entrance. Accommodation was to be made for 1000 rounds a gun and communication trenches dug between the gun pits and the dug-outs.

All this work was done during the day without hindrance of any kind from the enemy. This was due entirely to the splendid patrol work of the RFC as no German plane was allowed to remain for any length of time over our lines.

15   The Brigade Ammunition Column ceased to be part of the Brigade, being absorbed into the Divisional Column as the 3rd section, A echelon, Divisional Column. Simultaneously, Batteries within the Division were reorganised. C Battery was transfered to the 97th Brigade, while C/97 (Howitzer Battery) became D/96 and D/96 in consequence became C/96 as GHQ had ordered the junior battery of each Field Artillery Brigade to be the Howitzer Battery.

97th Brigade RFA, War Diary 1916
May 1916; Lt Colonel Pottinger;
DERNANCOURT; Map 62d NE 1/20000

20   Reorganisation of Brigade A/97 becoming D/95, B/97 becoming D/94, C/97 becoming D/96 while A/95 became A/97 preparing positions at F1b.70.36. B/94 became B/97 in action at F19a.4.5 (under 94th group) C/96 became C/97 with 1 section in action at F7a.0.4 (under 96th group) and one section in action at E11a.3.7 (under 94th Brigade group).

22   Lt JR GREIG A.V.C. transferred to Divisional Transport. Lt WALL A.V.C. attached to 97/RFA. Construction of the Brigade battle HQ discontinued and work on Divisional OP continued until end of month.

27   A/97 relieved C/95 at E12b.6.3 (counter Battery group).

28   C/95 relieved B/97 at F19a.4.5 (under tactical command of 95th group).

31   2/Lt TEGETMEIER rejoined Brigade.

June 1916; DERNANCOURT; Map 62d NE 1/20000

3   Lt TEGETMEIER attached to A/97.

5   New Battle HQ commenced at F7a.6.3.

13   9.30pm - one section of A Battery moved from E12b.6.3 to F1b.70.36 taking their guns from wagon lines.
         6pm - one section B relieved one section A Battery at E12b.7.3. Gun exchanged.

14   9.30pm - remainder of A Battery moved to new position taking guns from wagon lines.
         6pm - remainder of B Battery moved from wagon lines to relieve A/97 at E12b.7.3. Guns exchanged. C Battery taking their guns with them moved to F7b.38.52 - one section from E12a and the other from F7a.

15   Brigade Battle HQ at F7a.6.3 abandoned, falls having taken place 6 times. This is attributable to continuous wet weather and to the failure of the RE to supply the requisite material. New Brigade Battle HQ commenced at F7a.05.05. Work proceeded day and night.

16   Unloading of ammo at Batteries began this night.

21   Brigade HQ moved into Battle HQ at F7a.05.05. Dressing station for Brigade established at same point.

22   Brigade OP established at F7a.8.5.

23   Brigade in position at following points to take part in Anglo-French offensive on the SOMME Brigade: HQ F7a.05.05, A Battery F1b.75.36, B Battery E12b.7.3, C Battery F7b.3.5, wagon lines at DERNENCOURT at E21c.6.4.
         Midnight - 1000 rounds per gun dumped at Batteries.

24-30   Brigade cooperated in bombardment as per *21st Division Artillery OO No 22* (map of MONTAUBAN 1.20000) On 30th, Infantry Brigadier concurred report that they were satisfied that the enemy's wire had been sufficiently destroyed. Expenditure of ammunition from 24th–30th 10946 A, 6013 AX. Casualties - officers nil, OR killed nil, wounded 3. So far the equipment has stood the task well but signs of spring trouble. Batteries report that guns are still shooting accurately.

July 1916; BECORDEL

War diary destroyed by shellfire

[As the above diary was destroyed, the 94th Brigade diary is used for continuity.]

94th Brigade RFA, War Diary 1916
July 1916; Colonel F M Banister; BECORDEL

1   All map references on MONTAUBAN and MARTINDUICH 1:20000.

6.25am - commencement of concentrated bombardment in accordance with *21st Div Instructions for Offence No 4.*

7.30am - 63rd and 64th Infantry Brigades attacked enemy front line (with 50 Brigade of 17th Division). The aim was to clear front system of enemy trenches on right flank of assaulting troops and to occupy a position near RIO COTTAGE.

2.30pm - attack on FRICOURT preceded by a 30 minute bombardment. Attack held up by machine guns in craters.

2   12pm - attack due on FRICOURT was cancelled when our men reported seen in enemy trench. Brigade ordered to barrage from F4a.05.80 along track running to FRICOURT FARM. Infantry advanced with no opposition to a line from X28c.1.4 to POODLES at 1.26pm.

1.15pm - A Battery ordered to BECORDEL; other Batteries to Battery position.

9.15pm - A Battery ordered to return to BELLEVUE FARM; teams of other Batteries to wagon lines.

3   9am - A Battery ordered up to BECORDEL VILLAGE. Positions near SUNKEN ROAD reconnoitred. Attack not sufficiently advanced to allow Batteries to be taken up. A Battery moved up to X27d.2.1.

8.15pm - A Battery in action - registered.

4   Batteries near X27d and F5a.

5   *21st DA MB 407, MB 412* Orders to search CONTALMAISON at slow rate of fire for 30 minutes (B, C and D Batteries and A & C Batteries 79th Brigade).

10pm - orders for night firing on CONTALMAISON and BAZENTIN LE PETIT.

6   Batteries did not fire.

7   1.25-2am - search trench running west of CONTALMAISON X16d.5.1 to X16b.1.4 *21st DA OO 23,* 52nd Brigade attack on PEARL ALLEY. Reported attack failed. Bombardment carried out. *para 7 of OO 24.*

8pm - attack on QUADRANGLE SUPPORT TRENCH - ACID DROP COPSE and strip of wood between WOOD TRENCH and WOOD SUPPORT. Tasks as laid out in *BM 472* at 7.30pm.

8   5.50pm - attack on flank of QUADRANGLE SUPPORT and junction of PEARL ALLEY, and junction of PEARL ALLEY and QUADRANGLE SUPPORT. *21st DA OO 25.* A Battery at MIDDLE ALLEY, D Battery at WOOD TRENCH.

9   2pm - enemy shelled heavily from north of SHELTER WOOD to OVILLERS and our trenches from BOTTOM WOOD to QUADRANGLE. Two Batteries turned onto WOOD TRENCH SUPPORTS.

10   3.30am - bombardment of south and south-west portions of MAMETZ WOOD *21st DA OO 27, 10th July 1916.*

11pm - batteries ordered to occupy forward positions. The approach was being shelled along SUNKEN ROAD. C Battery into position between LOZENGE WOOD and LONELY COPSE. B Battery to original position.

11 A and C Batteries wire cutting from forward positions S13b.7.7 to S13b.4.9. A, B and C Batteries took up forward positions along a hedge running from SHELTER WOOD to BOTTOM WOOD in X28b. D Battery at F5a.3.8.

12 Wire cutting from S13b.7.7 to S13b.4.9. Zone kept under fire during the night.

10.30pm - concentrated bombardment on BAZENTIN LE PETIT WOOD for 5 minutes.

13 Bombardment of zone continued. S13b.7.7 to S13b.4.9.

14 *21st DA OO 27* Attack on BAZENTIN LE PETIT WOOD.

3.20am - bombardment of front line.

3.25am - barrage lifted and Infantry attacked. Attack successful and wood taken.

12.35pm - ordered to fire continual bursts of fire 300 yards clear of north-west corner of BAZENTIN LE PETIT WOOD. Night firing on square M32.

15 11am - barrage 300 yards clear of north west edge of BAZENTIN LE PETIT WOOD. Section fire 30 secs. [*MB 638*].

1.35pm - ordered to shell Rly [Railway??] from S8a.12.60 to S2c.10.40 with A, B and C Batteries and D Battery to engage enemy guns reported at S8a.4.6.

1.48pm - above orders cancelled. Night firing as laid out in *MB 662* - southern boundary of zone S1d.5.8 to S2c.0.8.

16 10am - orders to search for wire in front of SWITCH TRENCH S1b.5.1 to 2a.10.75. Night firing same.

17-19 Bursts of fire on SWITCH TRENCH.

20 *21st DA OO 29.* 2.55-4.25am - bombarded SWITCH TRENCH from S2b.4.6 to M33c.0.0 to support an attack

by XV and XIII Corps. D Battery M33c.7.3 to M33d.25.20. Night firing on SWITCH TRENCH S2b.4.6 - M33c.0.0 (A B C Batteries). D Battery S2c.03.85 to S2b.4.6.

21 Night firing as above - A, B and C Batteries *21st DA OO 30.*

22 *21st DA OO 31* 3.20 - 3.30am - concentrated bombardment on SWITCH TRENCH M33d.25.15 to M33c.7.3.

7pm-1.30am - bombardment on zone S3b.80.85 to M33d.55.05 in support of attack by XIII corps on DELVILLE WOOD and III corps on SWTICH TRENCH on left of XV corps.

23 Night firing M33d.6.0 to S4a.0.7.

24 Brigade withdrawn and marched to BONNAY.

25 Marched to ARGOEUVRES.

26 Marched to BOURDON.

27 Marched to ST RIQUIER.

29 Marched to BEALCOURT.

30 Marched to LIGNY SUR CANCHE.

31 Gnr W RILEY (C) awarded Military Medal.

Cas 3 Gnr MORRIS (A) and Bdr SWINOLES (C) wounded.
4 Sgt BURNHILL (C) wounded.
6 Gnr BATTY (A) shell shock.
10 Sgt PORTER (A) and Gnr JARVIS (A) wounded.
11 Bdr JORDAN (C) and Sgt MYERS (C) wounded.
12 Gnr FROGGATT (B) and Gnr STEPNEY (C) killed. Gnr CAMPBELL (C) and Gnr HASELL (C) wounded.
14 Bdr BISHOP (B), Gnr MACKER (B), Gnr GRAY(B), Gnr HOLMSHAW (B) and Gnr SCRAGGS (D) all wounded.
15 Bdr CASWELL (C) and Gnr HASTILL (C) wounded.
16 Bdr ROYLE (B), Gnr MAWER (B), Gnr LAVER (B) and Gnr HOGG (A) wounded.
17 Dr McDONALD (D) wounded.
20 2/Lt WCA FREEMEN (A) and Gnr LAING (C) wounded.

97th Brigade RFA, War Diary 1916 August 1916; DENIER

1   Orders were received to move up to the ARRAS area to relieve 14th Divisional Artillery.

2-3   21st Divisional Artillery relieved 14th Divisional Artillery by sections and single guns (in case of detached sections). A/97 came under 95th Brigade group for tactical purposes, C/97 came under 94th Brigade group for tactical purposes, B/97 (less 1 section) came under 94th group for tactical purposes, B/97 1 section came under 96th group for tactical purposes. Batteries continued to be under 97th Brigade HQ for administration.

4   HQ 97th Brigade relieved HQ 49th Brigade at WANQUETIN. Lt Col POTTINGER was appointed Town Commandant of WANQUETIN with Lt REPEN as Town Major.

10   WANQUETIN 2/Lt FARRELL A/97 admitted to hospital suffering from trench fever.

25   Lt Col POTTINGER RFA left to take over command of 283rd Brigade RFA.

28   Maj MRC NANSON B/97, 2/Lt LANKTREE B/97 and Lt TB McLEROTH RFA left to join 11th Divisional Artillery. Reorganisation of 21st Divisional Artillery ordered.

30   Reorganisation completed: A/97 became A/95. B/97 (less 1 section) joined A/94 to make 6 gun Battery, B/97 1 section joined B/94 to make 6 gun Battery, C/97 less 1 section joined C/94 to make 6 gun Battery, C/97 1 section joined C/95 to make 6 gun Battery.

31   Lt F REPEN RFA attached to 21st Division Artillery (HQ) Lt NASH assumed duties of Town Major Adjutant. Orderly Officer and HQ staff. only (NCOs and men) left.

94th Brigade RFA, War Diary 1916 September 1916; Colonel F M Banister; ARRAS

3-9   Colonel FM BANNISTER to Divisional HQ during leave of GOCRA. Colonel ROUSE assumed command of 94th Brigade group.

8   Orders received for relief of the Brigade by the 159th Brigade.

9-10   Col BANNISTER returned. All Batteries marched to ETREE WAMIN.

12   Marched to SARTON and bivouaced.

13   Marched to BELLEVUE FARM arriving at 1.30pm. Sheet 57C SW 1/20000. Batteries went into action at square S16 during night. HQ in MONTAUBAN.

14   *41st DA orders no 10* received to attack on 15th with objective of capturing defences up to and including the line MORVAL-LES-BOEUFS - GUEDECOURT and HIGH WOOD. *41st DA No49.* Registration carried out.

15   *41st DA T26* .6.20am - attack by 124th Infantry Brigade on right and 122nd Infantry Brigade on left. 123rd Infantry Brigade in reserve. Attack progressed well.
       3.28pm - situation reported as line running north of COURCELETTE - north of MARTINDUICH down to HIGH WOOD. Some Germans still in HIGH WOOD. Line then north of M35 central to M36 central. FLERS line consolidated but situation obscure; probably in our hands. Our troops appear to have advanced beyond T8 central. "Tanks" first employed on this day - proved to be a success.

16   Attack continued on GIRD TRENCH and GIRD SUPPORTS in front of GUEDECOURT - not successful; line held same as 15th September.

17   4.40pm - orders received for Batteries to move forward. Positions reconnoitred and occupied S18c + d. HQ at S24a.1.8.

18   Registration carried out of GIRD TRENCH.

19-24   Continuous day and night firing.

25   *41ˢᵗ DA OO 17.* 12.35pm - attack on GIRD TRENCH and GIRD SUPPORTS (successful) and GUEDECOURT (not successful).

26   5.30am - attack resumed and GUEDECOURT was taken and consolidated through the day.

27   2.15pm - GIRD TRENCH and GIRD SUPPORTS from N26a.5.9 to N19b.3.2 attacked and objective gained. B and D Batteries ordered forward to near FLERS in S6 and T1a respectively.

28-30   Day and night firing.

Cas   14 Gnr A MARTIN (A) wounded Cpl R TURBITT (A) killed, Cpl H JORDON (A) wounded, Gnr G RICHARDSON (A) killed, Bdr P OAKLEY (A), Gnr J AIREY (A), Sgt E LACROIX(A), Gnr W BRUNDISH(A), Gnr TE LOWNDES(A), a/Bdr G CAMPEY (A) all wounded.
        15 Sgt J TURNER (C), Gnr JH WINTER (C) both killed, Gnr R TODD (C) wounded.
        16 Gnr JW ROBSON (C) and 2/Lt FO TRENCHMAN (A) wounded.
        17 Gnr JR THOMPSON (D) killed. Gnr AE WILSON (D), Fitter H MARTIN (D), Gnr J BARNARD (D), Gnr A HARRISON (D), Gnr W ELLIS (D), Gnr F REMINGTON (D), Bdr CA HUNTER (D) all wounded 2/Lt CFJ MALET VEALE (C) wounded in action.
        18 Gnr A LYMAN (A) wounded and Gnr E PETERS (A) killed.
        19 Gnr W BRUNDISH (A), Gnr RD SMITH (C) wounded.
        20 Lt L WEST (D) wounded.
        25 Gnr WN GIBSON (C) wounded, Gnr J LEWIS (C) wounded - accidental, self inflicted, Gnr H ARMSTRONG (D), Gnr F HESSEY (C) both slightly wounded, remained at action, Gnr S MARTIN (B), Bdr S POWELL (C), Lt JE MULLER (C) all wounded. a/Bdr J REED (D) wounded.

26 2/Lt ES DREW (C) killed, Gnr J JOHN (C) and Gnr G THOMAS (C) both wounded.

28 Dr C WILSON (D), Gnr T GURNETT (D), Dr H BESWICK (A) and Gnr ST PURDY (B) all wounded.

October 1916; Major WT Synnott; SOMME

1   *21ˢᵗ DA OO No4.* 3.15pm - Brigade task to barrage 250 yards in front of present line from N19b.45.88 - N19a.64.88 (GIRD SUPPORTS) in support of a NZ Division attack on GIRD LINE as far as M24b.0.5.

7.45pm - A and C Batteries moved to forward positions near FLERS, A in S6b and C in N31c respectively.

9.15pm - enemy appeared to be massing for counter attack. Rate of fire quickened for 30 minutes. Attack did not develop.

2   Day firing carried out. 12.35pm - barrage at 80 rounds per hour along east - west line from N13c.5.1 to N13d.5.1. Enemy reported to be making a trench. Night firing SOS line N15d.5.3 - N13c.5.0 - M24b.1.9 - M18c.0.4 - M17d.5.3.

3   *21ˢᵗ DA D48.* Quiet day with day and night firing.

8pm - received news that Division on left hold all EAUCOURT ABBE. Brigade HQ moved to FLARE TRENCH in S12b.

4   4.40-4.45pm and 5.08-5.20pm - heavy enemy shelling at our trenches at SUNKEN ROAD in N19b. Batteries opened fire on SOS lines.

6.30pm - heavy enemy shelling north of GUEDECOURT.

5   Day and night firing carried out. C Battery position shelled by 8″, 5.9″ and 4.2″. Detachments had to be withdrawn (3 killed and 5 wounded OR).

6   3.15pm - commencement of bombardment in accordance with *21ˢᵗ DA OO no 5.*

7   1.15pm - infantry attack on BROWN LINE. Infantry advanced to first crest but held up by machine gun fire from right flank. By late evening Infantry wire reported 300 yards in front of original line.

8   7.45am - ordinary day firing commenced.
     9.15am - line given N19b.4.6 - N19a.5.9 - N13c.00 - M24b.4.7 - M24a.8.6 - M17d.9.1.

9   Battery shelled trenches in zones all day.
     6.10pm - heavy enemy barrage along whole front. Batteries opened fire on SOS lines. No action resulted and SOS call reported not confirmed.
     6.20pm - fire practically died away.

10   Ordinary day and night firing carried out.
     12.40pm - JUICE ALLEY reported full of Germans. All Batteries turned on this.

11   7am - bombardment of BAYONET TRENCH - JUICE ALLEY - LIME TRENCH. *21st DA OO no 6.* C Battery badly shelled and withdrew to S6b.8.1. (4 killed and 8 wounded OR).

12   2.05pm - Infantry attack on BROWN LINE - not gained *(21st DA 00 no 7).*

13   Ordinary day firing carried out. Sections of A B C D and B/96 relieved by 62nd Brigade (and sections of A/64th to B/96th) RFA; marched to wagon lines.

14   Sections relieved and marched to BONNAY. Command passed to 62nd Brigade. 8.30pm - remaining sections relieved.

15   Remaining sections marched to BONNAY.

16   Marched to TALMAS; bivouaced for night.

17   Marched to AMPLIER.

18   Marched to BOUBERS SUR CANCHE.

19   Marched to BERGUENEUSE and EQUIRRE.

20   Marched to LAPUGNOY.

21   One section of each Battery marched to wagon lines of Batteries of 45th Brigade RFA and relieved.

22   Remaining sections relieved. Command of front QUARRIES sector taken over, Major SYNNOTT taking over from Lt Col HILL.

Cas   1 Gnr CE SCRAGGS (D) wounded.
2 Gnr JHC WORSALL (A) wounded and Gnr JF GOAMAN (A) killed. Gnr J COOPER (B) killed, Gnr T HODGSON (B), Gnr AJ THOMPSON (B), Dr G LEWISTON (B) all wounded. Lt B MULLHOLLAND (D) wounded, Bdr A LONGMAN (D), Sgt R GRISTWOOD (D) both killed, Gnr DC MONTMORENCY (D), Gnr G WALLACE (D), Gnr A HARRISON (D), Gnr H BENNETT (D), Gnr G MORGAN (D), Gnr AG MYNER (D) all wounded.
3 Gnr W CADDY (A) admitted to hospital with smashed leg, Cpl J HARDING (A) wounded.
4 Bdr W BUDGE (C), Gnr W SOUTHALL (C) and Dr SLOAN (D) all wounded.
5 Gnr B BOYD (A) wounded, Dr RUTHERFORD (A) reported missing. Gnr W GLEN (C), Gnr C MONK (C), Gnr T ROBINSON (C) all killed. Gnr AH MILLER (C), Gnr J KNOX (C), Sgt A BIRD (C), Gnr T COLEMAN (C), Gnr JH SHELDON (C) all wounded.
6 Sgt F NICHOLSON (A) killed. Bdr JWT PLACE (A) wounded, Cpl C NICHOLSON (A) slightly wounded but remained at duty.
10 Bdr R UNDERWOOD (A) slightly wounded, remained at duty, Gnr M GIBBONS (A) killed. Gnr JH TAYLOR (C) wounded.
11 Sgt G BROWN (A) wounded, Dr JH MARROW (B) reported missing, Gnr JR BILSHAW (C) killed. Sgt SW MACKRILL (C), Gnr R DEMPEY (C), Gnr WE SHENTON (C) all wounded. Gnr J WHITHAM (C) wounded but remained at duty, Cpl DC SCOTT (C) killed, Gnr J TASKER (C), Gnr H WILKINSON (C) wounded.
14 Gnr N MORRIS (HQ) wounded but remained at duty.

November 1916; Colonel F M Banister; NOYELLES; Sheet 36c NW

6	D Battery bombardment of TM at H7a.20.25 *21st DA orders BM 231/2.*
7	Blew a mine at G11b.85.35. B and C Batteries barraged both sides of this. D Battery shelled trench junction G12a.10.87 and G12a.03.72.
8	1.05pm - bombardment of TM at G5d.60.45. *21st DA orders BM 231/8 of 7th.*
10	2/Lt EGJ DENVIR (A) awarded Military Cross.
15	12.30pm - bombardment of front line trench G5d.80.16 - G5d.9.2 by C and D Batteries Ref *21st DA Btn 231/2, 10th Nov 1916.*
18	5.15pm - bombardment of enemy trenches and tramway system round ST ELIE.
22	In cooperation with Trench Mortars, front and support trenches from G12a.9.1 - H13a.3.9 were bombarded.
24	Bombardment of trench from G12b.48.15 - G12b.38.25 *Ref 21st DA Btn 231/2, 19th Nov 1916.*
25	Cpl IA GARNER (A), Cpl C NICHOLSON (A), Dr CE CAYGILL (A) Sgt TH ROBERTS (C) all awarded Military Medal.
27	Bombardment of GTE ST ELIE and trenches G12b and d by 1st corps Heavy Artillery of 94th and 95th Brigades. During this D Battery had a premature in bore. This killed 1 and wounded 3 and destroyed the gun. Capt AC Mac G TAYLOR joined and posted to C Battery.
Cas	7 Gnr R ROSS (B) killed by falling off partially ruined wall. 27 a/Bdr DR WILLIAMS (D) killed and Sgt W DAVIS (D), Gnr WAGSTAFF (D) and Gnr J OSBORNE (D) wounded by premature.

December 1916; Lt AP Turner; QUARRIES sector; Sheet 36c NW

3   Gnr MUGGLESTON (D) awarded Military Medal.

11   Final shoot of enemy trench tramway system *ref 21 DA Btn 231/2.*

14   Brigade shot on enemy trenches and defences north of ST ELIE in H1d.

16   Bombardment of enemy works at the SALIENT G12d.5.8. *21st DA OO No5.*

20   Bombardment of enemy defences from H7c.0.3 - G12d.80.67. *21st DA OO No6.*

23   Enemy bombardment of our trenches in morning using field guns and trench mortars. Divisional Artillery carried out concentrated bombardment in retaliation.

24   A Battery position badly shelled (2 officers 1 OR killed, 3 OR wounded).

24-26   Irregular shelling of enemy trenches.

Cas   7 Sgt A INCE (AVC Attached), Bdr W BURKE, Gnr AGNES (attached to C from 35th Am SP) all wounded.
         23 Gnr G CARLING (A) wounded.
         24 2/Lt PHS BEZUNDENHOUT (A), 2/Lt CBO BEUTTLER (A), Bdr S BAKER (A) killed, Sgt GW SADLER (A) wounded, Gnr A MARSDEN (A), Gnr H THORPE (A) wounded but returned to duty.

Chapter 6
Passchendaele 1917

The General Situation, Early 1917

By the start of 1917 the First World War had lasted nearly two and a half years. Millions of men on both sides had been killed or wounded. Conscription had started in Britain in 1916 after the supply of volunteers had dried up and women had found some new freedom taking on jobs previously held by men now fighting in the trenches. A major political change had also occurred; in December 1916 Herbert Henry Asquith, who had been Prime Minister since 1908, was ousted by David Lloyd George. Asquith, who had lost a son during the Battle of the Somme, was widely blamed for the failures of the war over the previous two years and was frequently attacked in the media. As a result, he had lost the drive and energy needed to be a successful war leader. Lloyd George, on the other hand, was charismatic and was seen as a man of action; as Minister of Munitions he had solved the problem of the amount of shells which failed to explode. Increasingly unhappy with the way Asquith was running the war, he formed a new coalition and proved to be a capable wartime leader, despite being in frequent conflict with Sir Douglas Haig.

The situation on the home front was worsening but tolerable; there were some shortages but Britain's control of the seas meant that supplies generally did get through. However in Germany the blockade of the Baltic ports had resulted in shortages in that country leading to hunger-related diseases such as rickets, scurvy and tuberculosis and a 50% increase in deaths amongst women and children.[1]

The Germans, eager to inflict a similar fate on Britain had deployed U-Boats to attack vessels in the Atlantic. In 1915 they sank 885,471 tons of shipping, and in 1916, 1.23 million tons.

This shipping included American vessels one of which was a liner named the Lusitania sunk in 1915. This loss resulted in the deaths of over 1,000 civilians.[2]

In the United States, officially neutral, President Wilson had been making efforts to secure peace and these efforts continued until early 1917. However, pressure had been growing on him to join with the Allies and the German escalation of its submarine warfare in January 1917 caused Wilson to break off relations with Germany. In the following months the Germans, thinking war with the USA was certain, sent a telegram to the Mexican Government proposing an alliance in support of Mexico reconquering territories it had formerly owned in Texas, New Mexico and Arizona. This telegram was intercepted by the British and once its contents were revealed to the US Government, American involvement in the war became inevitable, although it would be a long time before US troops landed in France.

On the battlefield tactics were changing. The Germans, who had decided that the huge losses they had sustained during the Battle of the Somme should be avoided, retreated 25 miles to previously prepared positions, which the British called the Hindenburg Line, in March 1917. As they retreated they burned houses, slaughtered livestock and poisoned wells to the extent that the British and French armies took over 900 square miles with not one building standing.[3] The new lines they had prepared were of a different style and required fewer men to defend them but they were still on high ground and therefore difficult to attack.

Meanwhile the British were continuing to develop tanks and their skills in artillery. By 1917 guns and ammunition were plentiful and more reliable and improvements in sighting objectives, for example through better mapping and observations from aircraft, resulted in more accurate shooting. New artillery tactics, such as the use of the Creeping Barrage - an advancing line of gunfire which infantry could walk behind until nearly in the enemy lines, first used by the British during the Battle of the Somme – were also being perfected.

The Battle of Arras, January - September 1917

Winter was a quiet time on the Western Front and Jack spent much of January and February 1917 in the front line in the area around Béthune, although not actively taking part in a great deal of action, or in billets in a rest area. That this was a quiet time is clear from the fact there were no casualties at all in his Brigade during these months. Conditions at the time were good for the men but horses were not so well accommodated:

> *Billets for men good generally. Horse standings are non-existent and much work will have to be done to make them. No overhead cover for horses in any case.*[4]

The weather was cold that winter and Jack's letters refer to this:

> *We are having some cold weather just now about three inches of snow, and hard frosts.*[5]

He is very grateful for the news and home comforts which family and friends send him - he mentions food parcels, cards, newspapers, postal orders and best of all a cardigan:

> *The cardigan jacket fits me like a glove and I tell you it is better than the army issue for warmth.*[6]

In March, his brigade was ordered to move south and, after a march of about 57 miles, the men arrived in the area west of Arras. After some time to rest and prepare positions the brigade went into action at the end of March near Boisleux Au Mont.

In April and May Jack was involved in the various Battles of the Scarpe which were part of the Arras Offensive. In these battles the 94th Brigade was in almost continuous action, although we know his battery had a few days rest at the end of May. During these battles Jack had a lucky escape. He wrote to his parents:

> *One of old fritz's shells dropped about four yards from me the other day and a piece of shrapnel cut a bit right out of my steel helmet fortunately I was none the worse only a little shook up.*[7]

The same letter, sent on 17th April, makes it clear that food supplies were irregular:

> *When you send the parcel send a bit of bread. we have been on bicuits for ten days without bread.*[8]

The Senior Supply Officer's diary confirms this:

> *1st April - Roads very bad owing to traffic and weather making transport difficulties very great*
>
> *8th April - Iron rations issued* [which would include the biscuits Jack refers to] *to whole Division and iron oat rations for all animals. Rum issue to Division. Weather very cold*
>
> *18th April - 70% fresh meat, no bread but biscuit. M & V* [tinned meat and vegetables] *in lieu of bacon, figs in lieu of vegetables*

After this things did start to improve and on 19th April each man was given 1½ oz. orange, ½ oz. figs in lieu of onions. The artillery must have been working hard because on that day they received a full rum issue whereas the infantry only got half their normal amount!

On 4th May the division were treated to some fresh vegetables:

> *Made arrangements to issue kale to the Division, a large field being found in the neighbourhood with no owner*

Despite this the army must have been worried about the lack of vitamins in the diet and from 12th May lime juice was issued three times weekly. Despite the monotony of the food given to the troops there was an occasional treat - although not this time for the artillery!

> *28th May - 12000 pieces of chewing gum drawn to be issued to Infantry Brigades.*[9]

Embroidered card sent home from Arras by Jack

The Arras Offensive was a joint effort with the French who were attacking further south near the River Aisne. The British attack around Arras on 9th April was preceded by a five-day bombardment during which a total of 2,800 guns were used.[10] Initially the British had some success and in some areas infantry troops advanced over three miles, the biggest advance since trench warfare began.

However, in the south, in the area covered by the 94th Brigade, very little progress was made.

Further to the north, Canadian troops were having more success and took the strategically important Vimy Ridge on 12th April. A further attack was launched on 23rd April. Although in some areas a further mile of ground was captured, the 94th Brigade War Diary reports that :

> Infantry failed to meet objectives and were back at original lines about 2.00pm.
> 6.00pm - Attack renewed with same objectives; again driven back and due to an enemy counter attack we were driven back and occupied a line as previous to morning attack.[11]

Another attack was ordered by Haig on 3rd May which again failed to meet its objectives, and thereafter fighting continued sporadically until the end of May when the offensive was abandoned. Although casualties in the 94th Brigade were not heavy during this time, the average daily loss rate for the fighting divisions as a whole between 9th April and 17th May was just over 4,000 men. This was a higher average than that of the Battle of the Somme a year earlier.[12]

Sometime during the Battle of Arras, at the end of April or beginning of May, Jack was promoted to Bombardier. He wrote home on 10th May:

*You will see by the top I have been promoted to Bombardier,
so you will have to address my letters Bdr instead of Gnr. I
expect you know what a Bdr is. he wears one stripe.*[13]

As a Bombardier he would have been responsible for a section
of about 14 men as well as the necessary horses and wagons,
and his pay would have increased to 2s 3d.[14]

After a period of rest at the end of May, Jack remained in the
area around Arras until early September. During this time he
was only involved in minor attacks.

Belgium

On 6th - 7th September 1917 Jack's brigade was on the move
again, this time to a different country - Belgium. Much of this
journey of about 48 miles was completed by train and by 13th
September they were in position near Reninghelst, just south of
Poperinge, about five miles from Ypres. At first the 94th Brigade
was not involved in heavy fighting and in such circumstances,
soldiers were often given time away from the Front to visit
Poperinge. This town was behind the lines and was well-known
as a place where troops could go for rest and relaxation in the
many bars and estaminets (small, homely cafés run by local
people who served up welcome meals of egg and chips, served
with wine or beer). Also in Poperinge was Talbot House, the
famous club for soldiers of any rank, which was opened in
December 1915 by an army chaplain, the Reverend Philip 'Tubby'
Clayton. After the war this house gave its name to the Toc H
movement which still exists today and "strives to promote the
importance of bringing all sectors of society together, regardless
of culture, religion or race."[15]

Conditions in this part of Belgium were not good for Jack's
brigade. On 12th September the Commander of the 21st Divisional
Artillery wrote:

*Positions are not good, on bad wet ground with no
protection from shell fire. Much work requires to be done*

on them. The area is under a good deal of hostile shell fire already.[16]

During September and early October the 21st Division was involved in the Third Battle of Ypres, which lasted from 31st July until 10th November. In particular Jack was engaged in two battles, at Polygon Wood from 26th September to 3rd October and at Broodseinde on 4th October.

Haig's plan was to use the attacks around Ypres in the summer of 1917 to break the deadlock on the Western Front. As a precursor to the offensive, Messines Ridge was taken in June 1917 following a huge artillery bombardment and the detonation of a million pounds of high explosives in 19 specially dug mines under the German lines. The explosion caused by these mines could be heard in London, 130 miles away.[17] Two other mines were not detonated and their location was forgotten. One of these did finally explode in 1955, apparently killing a cow; the other is still buried under the fields of Flanders.

Following the success of this operation, the main assault began at the end of July after another artillery bombardment which began on 16th July, during which the British fired 4,500,000 shells into the carefully-layered German defences opposite Ypres. The bombardment did serious damage to the German positions but in the process destroyed the area's land drainage system.[18] Heavy rain fell in August and this flooded the damaged ground easily; despite some initial gains, progress in August was slow and most assaults ended in failure.

The battles at Polygon Wood and Broodseinde were more successful; the weather had improved and artillery barrages were effective so that by early October the British held part of the Ypres Ridge.

As the weather began to worsen. Haig decided to press on and allied troops started to move toward the village of Passchendaele.

Passchendaele

The final offensive of the Third Battle of Ypres was the assault on the village of Passchendaele. After the Somme, the Battle of Passchendaele is perhaps the best known event of the Great War for most British people. The name conjures up an image of thick grey mud, often knee deep or higher, through which men and horses had to struggle during the attacks of October and November 1917. Men who were wounded often drowned in the muddy ground where they fell. As Haig himself said in one of his despatches:

> *The low-lying clayey soil, torn by shells and sodden with rain, turned to a succession of vast muddy pools. The valleys of the choked and overflowing streams were speedily transformed into long stretches of bog, impassable except by a few well-defined tracks … To leave these tracks was to risk death by drowning, and in the course of the subsequent fighting, on several occasions both men and pack animals were lost in this way.[19]*

Siegfried Sassoon summed up the situation succinctly in his poem Memorial Tablet:

> *…I died in Hell*
> *(they called it Passchendaele)[20]*

Jack's brigade was involved in this battle from 12th October until 13th November. From the start conditions were bleak; it rained heavily and as a result roads were often impassable. Throughout October the Divisional Artillery Commander made frequent reference to this in his diary:

> *9th October - Information as to the situation was again hard to procure owing to the lack of communication by*

telephone with the infantry. What information was obtained came by carrier pigeon from FOO [Forward Observation Officers] *with the infantry.*

17th October - Great difficulty is experienced in moving guns out of position on account of the deep mud, water-logged shell holes and lack of proper roads or tracks from the Battery positions to the planked road in the rear.[21]

Troops holding the line in shell holes, Passchendaele 1917 (IWM CO. 2246)

By the end of the month Jack and his colleagues had been in the front line for nearly two months without real rest and the situation had deteriorated still further. The Divisional Artillery Commander wrote a long summary of the conditions as an appendix to his diary:

1. The artillery of the 21st Division is rapidly losing its efficiency owing to the following causes:

a) The long time they have been continuously in action on an offensive front, i.e. from 12th September to present date.

b) Heavy casualties

Since 12th September, 21st Divisional artillery have lost from various causes 26 officers and 504 other ranks and the deficiency now is 233 other ranks. This includes about 50 men who have been gassed and are now at the wagon lines, some of whom may be fit again in a few days. As a large percentage of the casualties consist of NCOs and gunners, the Batteries are now left with very few of their original detachments, and it is impossible under present circumstances to train the reinforcements, which usually consist of partially trained men.

c) Gas shelling at night

The Batteries are constantly shelled with gas by night. The detachments are necessarily scattered and are generally exhausted. It takes a long time to get about with the ground in its present state and there is consequently great delay in warning the men, which may account for some of the casualties; but the gas appears to hang about for hours and many men are gassed hours after the shelling has ceased, especially when they are called out at night for an SOS signal.

It is a question for consideration whether an aeroplane or balloon could not go up at night to locate the Battery firing gas shell and direct the fire of the Heavy Artillery on to them. The fire takes place in rapid bursts, so the Batteries could possibly be located.

d) Lack of accommodation at the Battery positions

This is being taken in hand, but it is a slow process with the roads in their present state, and the lack of labour. The Batteries are so under strength and are so continuously worked that it is very difficult to find working parties.

e) Lack of accommodation at the Wagon Lines Not one of the Batteries have been accommodated with huts for the men or standings for the horses. The men sleep in make-shift bivouacs which they have erected for themselves and sleep on the damp ground. The horses are standing up to their hocks in mud and are rapidly losing condition. An effort is now being made to make standings but the drivers are busy taking up ammunition and so labour is scarce. Heretofore no material has been available for standing and it was understood that they were being provided by the Corps, and now the ground is in such a state that fresh sites are required.

2. It is hardly surprising that, under these conditions the Batteries are not up to their former standard of efficiency. Even a week at their Wagon Lines does not help matters much, and I consider that they all require a month's rest out of the line to enable Brigade and Battery commanders to rest their men and reorganize their Batteries into really effective units.[22]

Despite such reports, which must have been received from more than one officer, the village of Passchendaele was captured by Canadian troops on 6th November and more of the ridge was secured in the following days. The hell that was Passchendaele did achieve some of Haig's objectives - the ridge was taken and the Germans no longer had the advantage of holding all the high ground in the area. However the main aim of breaking the deadlock was not achieved.

The Third Battle of Ypres was very costly with around 310,000 British casualties.[23] For the 94th Brigade of the Royal Field Artillery, October 1917 was the bloodiest month of the whole war; 170 men were reported wounded, mainly due to the effects of gas, and 23 were killed. Horses did not fare better; the divisional vets had to evacuate 497 horses between 2nd October and 15th November, mainly suffering from bomb wounds. These animals were transported by road, train or on horse floats. Also evacuated were 57 horse hides, presumably from horses which had died or had to be destroyed.[24] The suffering of Jack and his comrades is almost impossible to imagine and yet, as soon as the battle was declared over, instead of being given the rest recommended by the Divisional Artillery Commander, they were ordered back to France. Despite just leaving one of the most challenging environments imaginable, Jack's brigade undertook the journey of 53 miles over five days on foot, arriving at position north west of Arras on 19th November.

Horse struggling through mud near Passchendaele, October 1917
(IWM E(AUS).963)

Home on Leave

All through the summer Jack's thoughts were on the possibility of going back to Bilsdale on leave. He first mentioned this in a letter to his parents on 8th June and then again on 8th August and 10th September until on 17th October he wrote:

I am now No 6 on the leave list so I wont be long now if all goes well. I will let you know later on, when I am likely to be coming, so don't get worried, I shall not drop in as same as I did last time.[25]

There is no evidence to tell us when the "last time" was - there is no reference to any other leave in his letters so perhaps it refers to his pre-embarkation leave in the summer 1915.

After the hell of Passchendaele, receiving his leave papers must have seemed like a sign from heaven. The average length of leave at the time was ten days including travelling time so Jack probably left the front around 31st October. He seems to have travelled straight to Bilsdale and spent the first few days there. During this time he had a photograph taken. This shows both his bombardier's stripe and also a pace stick under his arm indicating that he may have taken a drill instructors' course.

Jack as Bombardier, 1917

Many years after the war, his brother Harry and sister Gladys used to speak about Jack seeming very depressed and fatalistic during his time at home, and the family began to wonder if they would see him again. Given what he had experienced in the previous months and years, it is easy to understand why such a fatalistic attitude could develop.

His letters show that towards the end of his leave Jack travelled to Nottingham to visit his cousin Bob, wife Ada and his sister Hannah who now lived with the couple. He arrived on 7th November and the next day was given a tour of the city including the Castle and the famous Jerusalem public house carved out of the rock face. He also went to the cinema. Sadly, this short time of "normal" life could not continue and at 1am on the morning of 9th November he travelled to Folkestone from where he embarked for France. On 10th November he was back with his brigade. Although he says he has "arrived once more safe and sound in France" it seems likely that Jack actually arrived in Belgium and moved south to Arras with the rest of the brigade a few days later.

After this journey some rest time was provided for the men, and but by the end of the month they were ordered south and, after another 40 miles of marching, Jack's unit arrived at positions between Roisel and Epéhy on 3rd - 4th December 1917. Parts of this journey must have been difficult, as the diary records:

1st December - Bivouacs in field. Weather very cold and insufficient tents provided

Although the next day things were somewhat better:

2nd December - Bivouac - covered standing for horses and Nissen huts for personnel.[26]

The weather deteriorated as December progressed but just before Christmas Jack received several food parcels and cards from his family:

Your cake was very good, and I am keeping Harry's peaches till Xmas day which I hope we shall enjoy very much. I thank Jane very much for her chocolate it was very nice, and very good of her I'm sure. Gladys sent some nice rice cake. I don't know whether she made it herself or not but it was fine. Some of my mates thought they had some fine cake, but it could not touch it as they said so themselves. We are having Xmas weather here just now. Snow on the ground and some severe hard frosts.[27]

The Senior Supply Officer was also doing his bit to ensure the men were able to have a treat:

23rd December - Drew 1½lbs Christmas pudding per man ... Rum issued to all.[28]

The battles of 1917 had resulted in 860,000 British casualties for virtually no territorial gain – about five miles at Arras and a similar amount around Ypres.[29] When Jack sent the card below to his family he, like everyone else, must have hoped that 1918 would bring an end to hostilities. As we now know, this wish came true but Jack would not live to see the victory for which he had fought.

Christmas card sent by Jack to his family, December 1917

Letters 1917

1. Post Card/21ˢᵗ Birthday Card from Gladys to Jack [January 1917]

To dear Jack with much love and "best wishes" for a Happy Birthday & many more to come From his Loving Sister Gladys

2. Postcard from Stockton sent from Norman Foulger to Jack [January 1917]

Dear Jack

Just a line to wish you many happy returns of Your 21ˢᵗ Birthday Hope you are quite well I received the cards all right thanks very much for them I will rite in a day or so and will tell you all news from Yours ever aff friend

Norman A Foulger (xxxxx)

3. Letter from Jack to Mary Emma and Isaac [January 21ˢᵗ 1917]

My Dear Mother and Father

just a few lines to let you know that I am still alive and well and in the best of health you would think me a long time in writing didn't you. We haven't had time to write lately. I wish this war was finished "don't you" I don't think it will last much longer but you can't tell. I received your parcel on the 15ᵗʰ Jan it had been knocked around a lot the cake was alright but the mince pie was all broken up That is the first one I have had so much damaged, but I enjoyed very much. I received your letter on the 10ᵗʰ I had a small parcel from Mrs Bennison which I have to acknowledge yet. I didn't receive any parcel from Chop Gate at New Year. I received two nice cards from Gladys and John and two from Mrs Foulger & Norman. We are having some cold weather just now about three inches of snow, and hard frosts. I Trust you all are keeping well and in the best of health as it leaves me in the pink. As Ed joined up yet I received his Xmas Card I had nearly forgot about it. So now I will close with all best wishes from your ever loving son

        J. W. Garbutt

               My best respects to Arthur

                  Bon Soir

4. Letter from Jack to Mary Emma and Isaac [February 17th 1917]

My Dear Mother and Father

  I now take pleasure in answering your last and ever welcome letter. I was pleased to hear that you were all keeping well I have received a letter from cousin Bob and also a photo of Hannah. Dosen't she look well I didn't know her till I read the letter. Let me know how Ed gets on the 20th I received your paper and Arthurs John Bull which interested me very much. You say Bob and Ed want to send me a cardigan Well I would be very pleased to have it. I have got one, and another would come in very useful for a change, because we have to wash them now and again. I think that is all, So now I will close with love and best wishes from your ever loving Son

        J. W. Garbutt

           xxxxxx

               I send my best respects to Arthur

  [on the back]

  I am quite well and in the best of health, and hope these few lines will find you the same

        Bon Soir

5. Letter from Jack to Mary Emma and Isaac [March 20th 1917]

My Dear Mother and Father

I now take pleasure in answering your ever welcome letter and parcel I recieved safe and sound on the 17th. The cardigan jacket fits me like a glove and I tell you it is better than the army issue for warmth. You ought not to have bothered with it when you had so much difficulty in getting one, and especially when poor little Harry was laid up seriously ill as he was. I would not have mentioned it in my letter only I thought Bob had it ready for you to send off. I was upset when I heard Harry had been so ill but I hope the poor little kid his recovering alright again I had a letter from Bob and he says he is getting better again. I didn't know Ben Cousans had been ill, but I thought it was a funny thing that I hadn't seen him on the march. I thought he looked badly that night when I saw him. Had Bob of cock flat any think to say about Canada Gladys says he as got a lot of swank since he has been away perhaps too much when he lost his stripes. What do you think of the British progress on the somme now it will be better in the future. I hope these few lines find you all well as it leaves me at present So now I will close with love and best wishes from your ever loving Son

　　　J. W. Garbutt
　　　　　Excuse scribble I haven't had much time
　　　　　　Bon Soir

6. Letter from Jack to Gladys [Good Friday, probably 1917]

Dear Gladys

I recieved your ever welcome letter this morning I was delighted to hear from you again. I hope you all are well as it leaves me in the best of spirits. As you say we are having a little *[censored]* now, but the weather is very wet at present and there is a good deal of mud about. Well I hope it will pick up a bit shortly. I haven't got much to tell you this time as their is not much worth writing every thing is just the same over and over again. I hope they are well at home Well I hope you have enjoyed your Easter as it did not trouble us much out here. I must conclude with love and best wishes from Your ever loving Brother

     J.W. Garbutt

7. Letter from Jack to Mary Emma and Isaac [April 17ᵗʰ 1917]

My Dear Mother and Father

  just a few lines in answer of your ever welcome letter I recieved yesterday 16ᵗʰ. Arthurs P.O. reached me safely. I was just beginning to wonder if you had recieved my last letter as it seemed such a long time since I heard from you, and above all I always like to receive my letter from home first, especially in a place were we are now. It is hell on earth at times. One of old fritz's shells dropped about four yards from me the other day and a piece of shrapnel cut a bit right out of my steel helmet fortunately I was none the worse only a little shook up. You upset me when you said Father was very bad. A (Jack=Johnson) wouldn't hurt me more, if their was anything happened to you or Father whilst I am out here miles away from home. I hope dear Dad you will soon be alright again and nothing may happen or trouble you till I come home again. I was mad when I heard uncle George had begrudged you a day or twos work from Ed. I know they are a mean lot and so is that other little devil at the Mill. They are all for them selves I'm alright to hell with you thats the way they carry on. I was so glad Harry had got out of hospital. I got your Papers safely. When you send the parcel send a bit of bread. we have been on bicuits for ten days withou bread, and send a card of Bull dog buttons. Well I think that is all trusting these few lines will find you all well and in the best of health as it leaves me A.1. So with best wishes and kisses I am your loving Son

J.W. Garbutt

Mrs Stephenson said I had to send you this page on out of the Christ. Hld. My best wishes to Arthur. I thank you very much for the P.O. I am longing for the time when I can come and shoot you a few more rabbits. I say don't kill them all leave a few for when I do come. I hope it won't be long. with love from

Jack

8. Letter from Jack to Gladys [April 20th 1917]

Dear Gladys

just a few lines to let you know that I am still alive and quite well, and I trust these few lines will find you the same. I would have wrote before only I haven't had time. The weather here as been severe, but I think it is getting much better now. I haven't heard from Mrs Foulger for a few weeks but I expect they recieved my last letter safely. Well I think that is all so excuse short any spare time I will write you more. Accept best wishes from your loving Brother

J.W. Garbutt

9. Letter from Jack to Mary Emma and Isaac [May 10th 1917]

My Dear Mother and Father

just a few lines in answer of your ever welcome letter I recieved safely the other day. I was surprised when I heard I had got another young Brother, but I was only to pleased to hear you were alright again I was glad to hear Father was a little better. I shall never forget the cockflat company for being so unkind to you whilst everything was being at a standstill. We are having glorious weather out here now. You will see by the top I have been promoted to Bombardier, so you will have to address my letters Bdr instead of Gnr. I expect you know what a Bdr is. he wears one stripe. We had a Gunner in our lot got wounded with us and he is in the hospital now at Helmesley. Well I think that is all now hoping these few lines find you all well, as it leaves me in the best of health with best wishes from your loving Son

    J.W. Garbutt

        Just a xxxxxxxxx for Baby

Well what about calling it Stanley I think thats a nice name. (dont you)

10. Letter from Jack to Mary Emma and Isaac [June 8th 1917]

My Dear Mother and Father

just a few lines in answer of your ever welcome letter I was pleased to hear from you again and that you all were keeping well. I am glad Father is much better. We have had a heavy thunder storm hear to day but the weather is generally fine taken it on the whole. I was pleased to hear you have got the potatoes in, and more than pleased to hear about Joe at the Mill and company being done in for once. I will look Clary Lengs battery up now as I have got his Address. I think they are in our vicinity. I haven't heard from cousin Bob of Notts since I wrote last. Well I think that is all So now I will conclude with all my love and best wishes from your affec Son

    J.W. Garbutt

just a little xxxxxx for Stanley hope he keeps well. my love and best wishes to Arthur hope he is keeping well. I don't know when my turn will come for leave. I hope thes few lines find you all well, as it leaves me in the best of health.

    Bon Soir

11. Letter from Jack to Mary Emma and Isaac [June 27th 1917]

My Dear Mother and Father

just a few lines in answer of your ever welcome letter I recieved safely to day. I was pleased to hear from you again, and that all was well. I was pleased to hear Father was ever so much better, and old Ed has got the turves ready for leading. Well we have got grand weather out here for the crops showers occasionally and sunshine. I haven't seen Ben Cousans yet, I expect he will be in the same regiment. Nor have I seen Clary Leng yet. I had a nice parcel sent from Mrs Stephenson about a fortnight ago. It was sent while she was staying in Glossop in Derbyshire. I recieved the 2/6 P.O. alright. I shall have to write and thank Bob for it. Dont send any more as I dont need them now, being as I am getting extra pay for my stripe. Were I was getting 8/ a week, I am getting 15/ now. But we don't get paid every week sometimes not for a month and then we only get one weeks pay. So I must have a little sum in credit. I have got Arthurs P.O. yet the last one you sent, and it is such a job getting them changed now, were we are at present. I was pleased to hear that Gladys has got another place near home. Well I think I have told you all now so I will conclude trusting these few lines find you all well and in the best of health as it leaves me in the pink So with love and best wishes from your Affec, Son

      J.W. Garbutt

          xxxxxxxxx Stanley esg

  My love and best wishes to Arthur

      Bon Soir

12. Letter from Jack to Mary Emma and Isaac [August 8th 1917]

My Dear Mother and Father

just a few lines in answer of your ever welcome letter I recieved safely this morning. I was pleased to hear that you all were well again. I expect by the time you recieve my letter Cousins Ada, Bob, and little Hannah will be with you for a few days holiday. What a nice thing if I could only be with you at the same time. Well I wish them every good luck and I hope they will enjoy thenselves. I am sure little Hannah will if it is only home. I had a nice letter from Cousin Bob this morning and he said they were going on their holiday on Aug 11th. I don't know when I shall get my holidays their dosen't seem to be any chance yet. I might be lucky about Xmas. I had a nice letter from Aunt Lily the other morning, and she told me I was her nearest relative a soldier. It appears all the rest are sailor men, and she belongs to a sea faring family. I got those two P. Orders changed about a fortnight ago and just in time two for one of them. We are having rain weather here very dull through the days. I haven't heard from Gladys yet nor Mrs Foulger either. What do you think of the Russians. Aren't they doing very bad just now. Well I hope these few lines find you all well as it leaves me in the best of health Well I think I have told you all now as I am in a hurry Accept best wishes from your loving Son

J.W. Garbutt

just a xxxxxx for Stanley

My love and best wishes to Arthur

13. Letter from Jack to Gladys [August 10th 1917]

My Dear Gladys

How glad I was to hear from you this morning, after such a long silence Well I am pleased you like your new place but I didn't know you had left Broughton. It will be more lively at Middlesbro won't it. Enjoy yourself as much as possible, but beware, and don't get into bad company. Excuse me saying that but you don't know who you are running up against in these days. I hope the weather keeps fine for your bank Holiday at Broughton. The weather is sunny here to day, but very cloudy. Yes I am sorry for poor Mrs Foulger what a blow for her. I saw the news in the Darlington paper what Mother sent me. I had a letter from Elsie Foulger yesterday, to break the news. She said she couldn't explain how it had upset them all, especially her Mother and George's fiance. Excuse me, are you keeping company with John, You will be quite near each other now Elsie told me you had been there since you went to Middlesbro, and how well you had took to her friend, who is in service at Norton. Well I am quite pleased to hear it. I had a nice letter from Cousin Bob in Nottingham, and by his letter they will be having their holiday on August 11th. They are going up home for 3 or 4 days and them to the sea-side. I only wish I could have been there too, just to see little Hannah. I think all is well at home. Stanley is growing a fine boy. Now I think I have told you all, so will close hoping these few lines to find you quite well as it leaves me A.1. with love and best wishes from your Affectionate Brother

J.W. Garbutt

xxxxx

Bon Soir write Soon

[George Foulger, Private G E Foulger, B Company, 9th Bn Yorkshire Regiment, died 13/06/1917, son of George and Ada Foulger of 22, Howard Street, Stockton on Tees]

14. Letter from Jack to Gladys [September 10ᵗʰ 1917]

My Dear Gladys

just a few lines in answer of your ever welcome letter, which I recieved with the greatest of pleasure. I was pleased to hear you were keeping well. The weather here is great. I haven't heard from the Foulgers for a long time I do hope someone will let me know what is the matter I was pleased to hear your friendship with "John" was getting very strong now. I don't see any chance of any leave just yet, but I hope to be coming shortly. It is two years since we came out to France, it doesn't seem quite so long "dose it". I never thought I should be out here two yrs, and it looks as though we shall be out here another year or two yet Well I think that is all I am sick of writing about the war So now I will close trusting these few lines will find you are your fiance quite well as it leaves me in the best of health with love and best wishes from your Affectionate Brother

      J.W. Garbutt

         Bon Soir

            My love and best respects to John

15. Letter from Jack to Mary Emma and Isaac [September 28ᵗʰ 1917]

My Dear Mother and Father

I now take pleasure in answering your most ever welcome letter which I recieved with the greatest of pleasure on the 24ᵗʰ of Sept. I was very pleased to hear that you all were very well. I have had a few lines from Ana, and she is quite well. She dosen't write so dusty now, but her spelling is only moderate. I didn't no she was living at Sexhow till she wrote, and been there a 12 months too, "that's good anyway". I had a letter and parcel from Gladys on the 25ᵗʰ. She sent two pairs of nice warm socks two cakes two handkerchiefs writing paper and batchelors buttons, and she had done everything well too. She made the cakes herself, and they were great. I think she will be like you Mother she will make a rare cook. I think they are moving into another house shortly perhaps you will know all about it. I was pleased to hear you were getting on with harvest. This as been a great month for corn "as it not". I don't think we have had rain once this month out here. It is fine weather now and were are giving old fritz a hot time of it too. I recieved your papers alright. I haven't had much time to look at them yet. Well now I think I have told you all. I hope these few lines will find you all quite well as it leaves me A.1. now I will close with love and all best wishes from your Affectionate Son

    J.W. Garbutt

 A few xxxxx for little Stanley

    I received a pair of socks from Mrs Stephenson, so I am well off again for socks. My love and best wishes to Arthur, hope the time will soon come when I shall be ranging his fields with the little pop gun on my shoulder out for the day to kill rabbits etc.

    Bon Soir

16. Letter from Jack to Mary Emma [October 17th 1917]

My Dear Mother

    I now take pleasure in acknowledging your card and parcel that I recieved safely on the 15th. I was pleased to hear that you all were quite well. The cake was super and the biscuits and samlon were lion. You asked me if we got plenty of butter in the army. Well no, but we get plenty of margarine which is butter to us out here. We have been having some rough weather here lately plenty of rain and now there is tons of mud. Well I am now No 6 on the leave list so I wont be long now if all goes well.

I will let you know later on, when I am likely to be coming, so don't get worried, I shall not drop in as same as I did last time. Well I don't think the war is going to finish yet do you. Well I havent got much time to write much so will close now hoping these few lines find you all well as it leaves me in the best of health with love and best wishes from your loving Son
  J.W. Garbutt

 Many thanks to all for the parcel and my love and best wishes to Arthur

17. Postcard (of Boulogne) from Jack to Mary Emma and Isaac [November 8th 1917]

Dear Mother and Father
 I am enjoying myself a treat at Nottingham leaving here tonight and quite well. Hannah, Cousins Ada and Bob are quite well. My word Hannah as grown a *[illegible]* girl, and she is so nice too with best wishes from your loving son
  Jack

18. Postcard (of Folkestone) from Jack to Mary Emma [November 9th 1917]

Dear Mother
 just arrived at Folkestone Friday from Nottingham hope the war will soon be over with all best wishes from
  Jack

19. Postcard (of Folkestone) from Jack to Diana [November 9ᵗʰ 1917]

Dear Sister
  just arrived at Folkestone enjoying myself a treat with all best wishes from
        Jack

20. Letter from Jack to Mary Emma and Isaac [November 10ᵗʰ 1917]

My Dear Mother and Father
  just a few lines to let you know that I have arrived once more safe and sound in France. I am not sorry either for the journey is very long and tiresome. I enjoyed myself a treat at Nottingham. I missed Bob at the station, but I found my way into Smenton Dale all right. I had been there about five mins before Bob came. He said he could have kicked himself for missing me. They were very good to me, and Bob showed me round all day on Thursday he never went to work, he said he was going to have a days holiday when I was there. He went to his office twice and showed me a bit of his work in the morning. He showed me all round the Castle and the Public House caved in the Rock you know which one it is and one or two other places he showed me and then we went to the pictures in the afternoon all of us. Hannah would not call me any thing but uncle Jack, but I think she knew me all the same. I shouldn't have known her if I had met her out in the street, she as altered that much. She is still as bonny as ever. She is very clever too, and speaks so nice She as got the Nottingham twang off alright. I don't think she could have been in a better place, and Bob makes a lot of fuss of her, and so dose Ada. Ada and Bob gave me a send of on Friday morning at 1 o'clock. I wish I could have stayed there a few more days I would have enjoyed myself better Life is only

short now a days and time is precious isn't it. Jane can have one of those Photos but I want one of hers just for old times sake. They want one at Nottingham too, but send one to me first and then I will tell you if they are any good or not. Well I think I have told you all now I will close with best wishes from your loving Son

      J.W. Garbutt

          Good Bye and God bless you all till we meet again. My love and best wishes to Arthur, and also give my best respects to Atkinsons

21. Letter from Jack to Diana [November 11th 1917]

Dear Sister Ana

  just a few lines to let you know that I have arrived safely to my unit once more. I am not sorry that I am here for the journey is very tiresome It is a wet day for a start too. I enjoyed my little self a treat at Nottingham while I was there. Cousin Bob was very kind and showed me all round. My word our Sister Hannah has grown a fine girl and speaks so well. I was very glad to see her. Well I will close with love and best wishes from your Affec Brother

      J.W. Garbutt

22. Letter from Mrs Hodgson to Mary Emma [15th Nov 1917]

Greenfields
Hilton
Yarm

Dear Mrs Garbutt

  Thanks very much for John's photo and address which we received quite safely yesterday our people think it isn't like him but I tell them it is just like what he is now he has altered considerably since they last saw him. A few years make a great difference in the appearance of young people. John was always a fine lad, & the prayer of my heart is that he may be spared to grow in to equally as fine a man as he was a lad. We know they are surrounded by danger on all sides but we must not forget that there is a God above who over rules everything & there is a passage which says "he is more than all that can be against us." I never go to bed on a night but I ask Gods blessing on our lads that are away, & while there are many going under I believe there will many come out safe in the end, for God will not let all our prayers be in vain, & I trust John may pull through all right. I fell there is great credit due to you both Father and Mother for turning our such a family, it shows they have had some good home training. I was away burying my Mother last Sunday. John would know her. I feel I've lost my best friend that ever I had for if ever anyone had a good Mother I had. It is also two years this weekend since I lost my brother. I must close now. With kind regards from us all.

> Yours faithfully
> MB Hodgson

23. Letter from Jack to Mary Emma and Isaac [November 21st 1917]

My Dear Mother and Father

I recieved your ever welcome letter this morning 20th, and also the cards. I mean the Photos, I don't reckon much to them. i was pleased to hear you all were well, but don't let it worry you about me, as I shall be alright. I am pleased to hear Ana as gone to live with Claphams she should be alright there. Send me Gladys address as I have lost it, and can't write till I get it. Give my best wishes to Arthur, Atkinsons and all the rest Well now I think I will close for the time being, hope these few lines find you all well as it leaves me in the pink. Accept best wishes from your loving Son

J.W. Garbutt

A xxxxxx for Stanley

Hope the war will soon be over, and all the lads safely back in Blighty

Bon Soir

de apre la guerre

take care of this letter *[written in a different hand, probably Mary Emma's]*

24. Letter from R Garbutt to Mary Emma and Isaac [25th Nov 1917] (son of George Garbutt and Margaret née Hoggart of Cockflat)

Somewhere in France

My Dear Ant and Uncle

I was so glad to hear from last night, so I must answer it right away, glad to hear you are all well, as this leaves me pretty Jake up to the present, considering - etc, as you say, glad Jack had a good time when home on leave poor lad I have tried to find them but failed (was) (but not now). As you say Mary I am trusting in God to help us, & best of all I expect to be on leave soon, some where just after Xmas, so I trust you are all living in hopes, for a good old time, I often hear from my dear sister Flor. What a pity, so near him & didn't see him, Now news are scarce, but perhaps I may have more when I get on leave so I trust you will excuse me Mary I am well and fat and look good too as usual, so I will now cut a long story short with kindest regards to all as ever and old Pal Bob & the rest

R Garbutt

25. Letter from Jack to Mary Emma and Isaac [December 22nd 1917]

My Dear Mother and Father

I now take pleasure in acknowledging your letters and parcel, which I have recieved safely. I was pleased to hear that you all were well. I recieved Arthur and Eds photo and also Jane's which I think is very good, and the other two have taken very well too. Well I have sent all the Xmas Cards I have got and hadn't enough to go round, so poor Arthur didn't get one "rather unlucky". Still I wish him a happy Xmas and ever prosperous New Year. You see we are in a place now were we cannot get Xmas cards, but I happened to get a few before hand. I have recieved Aunt Lily's parcel. A very nice parcel too, and a beautiful letter. I have also recieved Gladys parcel, and one from Mrs Stephenson and 11s 6d from Chop Gate, so I haven't done so dusty after all. Your cake was very good, and I am keeping Harry's peaches till Xmas day which I hope we shall enjoy very much. I thank Jane very much for her chocolate it was very nice, and very good of her I'm sure. Gladys sent some nice rice cake. I don't know whether she made it herself or not but it was fine. Some of my mates thought they had some fine cake, but it could not touch it as they said so themselves. We are having Xmas weather here just now. Snow on the ground and some severe hard frosts. I haven't heard anything from Cousin Bob since I came back of leave. Its a bad job for Joe at the Mill, although it perhaps saves him right in another way. I expect that is what he would have said if it had been any body else. Well I think I have told you all this time so will draw to a close wishing you all a happy Xmas, and ever prosperous New Year with all best wishes from Your loving Son

     J.W. Garbutt

       A Xmas xxxxxx to all

26. Letter from Jack to Mary Emma and Isaac [late December 1917??]

My Dear Mother and Father
    just a few lines to wish you all a happy New Year. I hope you have had a good Xmas. It as only been quiet here, but still I enjoyed myself the best way I could. I have recieved a letter, and Xmas Card from Jane. She as only put Jennie on her letter, so I cannot write back to her till I get her full name. I did know her name, but I have forgot it now, so please send it along in your next letter. I am sending you a New Year Card along with this, and hope you will get this alright I hope you are all well, as it leaves me in the best of health Snow is still on the ground here. I have recieved a 9s 4d P.O. from Fred W Pearson 52 Queens Road, linthorpe Middlesbro Perhaps you know some think about it Now I will close with all best wishes from your loving Son
        J.W. Garbutt

94th Brigade RFA, War Diary 1917
January 1917; Major WT Synnott;
NOYELLES; Sheet 36B 1/40000

3   Two sections of ABC and 1 of D Batteries relieved by 24th Brigade, 6th Division. Marched to RAIMBERT.

4   Remaining sections relieved and marched to RAIMBERT.

7   Sgt EC STOKOE (A) and Bdr T LIVERSEDGE (A) awarded Military Medal.

15   10pm - C and D Batteries sent to reinforce the line (under 24th Brigade Divisional Artillery). Were in action by daybreak of 16th.

19   C and D Batteries returned to training area at RAIMBERT.

23   *21st DA Instructions No1.* Orders for the relief of the 24th Divisonal Artillery by 21st Divisional Artillery received.

26   Brigade warned to be ready to march at an early hour tomorrow.

27   Map: HAZEBROUCK 5a. 5.50am - *21st DA OO No 11* received.

       9am - Brigade marched to NEUF BERQUIN went into billets.

28   Brigade marched to WATAU and billeted.

29-31 WATAU.

Cas   0

February 1917; Colonel F M Banister; WATAU

1-11 Billeted at WATAU.

12   Marched to HAZEBROUCK.

13   Marched to MT BERNENCHON.

15-16 Sheet 36C NW. Relieved sections of the 24th Brigade. Relief completed at 7.20pm on 16th. Batteries occupied same positions in QUARRIES sector as before.

22 Dummy raid in HOHERNZOLLERN sector. B, C and D Batteries operating.

Cas 0

March 1917; Colonel F M Banister; VERMELLES

4-5 Batteries withdrew to BELLERIVE. Positions remained empty with exception of C Battery which were occupied by C/95th Brigade.

6 Brigade HQ marched from NOYELLES to VERMELLES and joined Batteries at BELLERIVE. C Battery moved from BELLERIVE to MT BERNENCHON.

11 Brigade marched to BERGUENEUSE-ANVIN area.

13 Marched to BOURBERS SUR CANCHE.

14 Marched to LUCHEUX.

16 20 men per Battery formed a working party at DAINVILLE with 149th Brigade to prepare positions.

23 Sections of Batteries ordered to march to WAILLY; were recalled when on road.

26 Brigade marched to ADINFER WOOD and bivouaced.

27 Sheet 51B SW. Batteries in action at BOISLIEUX AU MONT. Brigade HQ to BOIRY ST RICTRUDE.

Cas 28 Bdr W JONES (D) wounded but remained at duty. 31 Bdr WR HESLYN (C), Bdr S GODDARD (C), Gnr W ELSON (C) all wounded, Gnr CLARK (C) wounded but remained at duty. Gnr PF TOMLIN died of wounds.

April 1917; Colonel F M Banister
BOIRY ST RICTRUDE; Sheet 51B SW 1/20000,

2 5.15am - attack on CROISILLES-HENIN road from T17c.70.05 to T3b.1.9 with 7th Division on right to attack CROISILLES and 30th Division on left to attack HENIN SUR CUJEUL. *21st DA OO No29.* 13th Northumberland Fusiliers

on right (T17c.9.2 to T10c.2.6) and 12th Northumberland Fusiliers on left (T10c.2.6 to T3a.4.2). Artillery support: Right group 95th Brigade / 291st Brigade RFA. Left group 94th Brigade / 290th Brigade and A/291 RFA. Objectives gained - 7th Division CROISILLES village; 30th Division HENIN SUR CUJEUL.

3-4   62nd Infantry Brigade relieved by 64th Infantry Brigade at T11c.0.4 - T3b.1.9. 3rd - Gnr AW CLARKE and BDR J PHIPPS (B) awarded Military Medal.

4-8   Bombardment of enemy defences prior to attack *21st DA OO 33 and 34.* Right group SENSEE river U7a.7.5 to T5 central to U2c.1.6 to N36b.5.4. Left group T5 central to HENIN-HENINEL road N34a.7.6 to N36b.5.4 to N29a.9.5. A/94 and A/291 detailed for wire cutting.

6   Sheet 51B SW. A/94 shelled, 1 killed, 2 guns damaged at T8c.3.3.

7   C/94 shelled, 1 killed, 2 guns damaged T20a.2.4.

9   General attack. 21st Division objectives *21st DA OO 36.*
1. Front line of German trenches T5a.5.2 to HENIN-HENINEL road.
2. 2nd line of German trenches T5a.7.7 to HENIN-HENINEL road.
3. Establish a line from N30c.05.90 to join present line at T10d.9.6.
4.15am - 64th Infantry Brigade (1st E Yorks on right, 15th DLI in centre and 9th KOYLI on left) attacked supported by 94th Brigade, 290th Brigade and A/291 on left with a creeping barrage in a line from T5c.7.9 - N34d.4.0 - N34c.8.6 - N34a.3.4 lifting at intervals until reaching N36a.3.4 - N29d.6.0 - N29a.7.0. 1st E Yorks achieved objective, others did not get through wire.
6.55pm - enemy counter attack drove right battalion out of front line trench. Line held at end of day T5a.5.3 to N34d.5.5.

10-12   Minor operations on HINDENBURG LINE by 64th and 62nd Infantry Brigade. Failed to gain objectives.

12   Attack arranged to capture first and second line trenches from T5a.45.22 to T4b.9.9 but these reported evacuated by patrols. *21st DA OO 39.*
11.35am - trenches occupied by 12th Northumberland Fusiliers on right and 13th Northumberland Fusiliers on left. Line held by 62nd Infantry Brigade that night was T10d.8.3 - T5a.45.22 - N35a.8.8 at which point in touch with 56th Division.

13   9.55am - attack held up by machine guns *21st DA OO no 42* and cancelled at 12.50pm. 62nd Infantry Brigade relieved by 19th Infantry Brigade at N33d.30.95 thro N34c, T5b, T5a and b on the road.

14   Attempted attack by VI and VII corps *21st DA OO 43* but little movement. Line held that night was N36a.7.7 - N36c.2.2 and from T6d.5.5 - T6c.7.5.

15-22   Bombardment of enemy defences *21st DA OO No 47-49.*

22   2.30pm - practice barrage carried out.

23   4.45am - attack by 33rd Division with 100th and 98th Infantry Brigade covered by 21st Divisional Artillery. Objective - parts of the HINDENBURG LINE between 80 contour and SENSEE river. *21st DA OO 49.* Infantry failed to meet objectives and were back at original lines about 2pm.
6pm - attack renewed with same objectives; again driven back and due to an enemy counter attack we were driven back and occupied a line as previous to morning attack.
Gnr A WHALLEY (A) awarded bar to Military Medal.

24-30   General bombardment on whole front *21st DA OO 51 - 55.*

30   Gnr TH WOOD (A), Gnr A FELDON (D), a/Bdr A GAMAGE (C), Bdr F PRIME (D) awarded Military Medal.

Cas   3 Gnr O MAYO (B), Dr TS BROWN (B) wounded.
6 Bdr J NORTON (A) killed.

7 2/Lt CGW DENVIR (A) wounded, Gnr H MOULD (C) killed, a/Bdr CJ SHARPE (C) wounded, Bdr J CREE (D) wounded.

9 Gnr W BAKER (C) wounded.

13 Lt PME BROWNLOW (?) (B) wounded, Gnr McBRIDE, Gnr MARRIOTT (D) wounded.

18 a/Bdr W FRANCIS (D) wounded.

20 Gnr AW POWE (B) wounded but remained at duty.

23 2/Lt EB REID (B) wounded by premature but remained at duty.

May 1917; Colonel F M Banister; BOIRY-BECQUELLE; Sheet 51B SW 1/20000

1 Gnr TH WOOD (A), a/Bdr A GAMMAGE (C), Bdr FM PRIME (D), Gnr A FELDON (D) awarded Military Medal.

2 Brigade HQ moved to sunken road T10c.0.8.

3 *21st DA OO 57.* Attack by 62nd, 64th and 110th Infantry on SENSEE RIVER/HINDENBURG LINE - unsuccessful. Positions at end of day: HINDENBURG front line as far as U1c.4.0. Support line to U1c.4.5 - 64th Infantry Brigade. SUNKEN ROAD from U1d.0.3 - Cross roads U1d.8.9 to WOOD TRENCH U2a.1.5 - 110th Infantry Brigade. 62nd Infantry Brigade as this morning.

10 D Battery withdrew to wagon lines for a rest.

10-11 21st Division (less artillery) relieved by 33rd Division.

12 21st Divisional Artillery relieved by 37th Divisional Artillery.

14 D Battery ordered into position again.

20 Map: CHERISY 1/10000 *39th DA OO 57.* 5.15am - attack on HINDENBURG LINE. 100th Infantry Brigade - line between CROISELLES HENDECOURT and CROISELLES - FONTAINE road. 98th Infantry Brigade - south east down

HINDENBURG LINE as far as CROISELLES - FONTAINE road. 19th Infantry Brigade - attacked the HUMP in U14c and form defensive flank from U14c.1.3 - to crossroads at U14c.2.9. Partly successful. 100th Infantry Brigade held front line held but not support line. 98th Infantry Brigade reached a point about 30 yards north of the river road in the supports and gained touch with the 100th Infantry Brigade at the FONTAINE-CROISILLES road.

7.30pm - continued attack. 98th - attack down HINDENBURG SUPPORTS to 100 yards north of SENSEE river. 19th - occupied shell holes about 150 yards this side of objective (line between NELLY LANE and FONTAINE-CROISILLES road).

24   a/Bdr T ROBSON (A) awarded Military Medal. Gnr E MEADS (A) awarded bar to Military Medal.

27   1.55pm - attack by 98th Infantry Brigade captured HINDENBURG support as far as LUMP LANE. Second attack by 19th Infantry Brigade failed and Infantry back in original line by 2.14pm.

29   C Battery withdrawn to rest camp.

31   21st Divisional Infantry relieved 33rd Divisional Infantry.

Cas   11 Gnr E MEADS (A) died of wounds, Gnr WH BERESFORD (B) wounded but remained at duty, Dr W CLEARY (C) killed, Dr WH EVANS (C) wounded as wagon lines were shelled at BOIRY BECQUERELLE.

19 Sgt HI JEFFERIES (C) wounded but remained at duty.

21 2/Lt EWC ARNELL (C) wounded.

24 Gnr F HARDY (C) wounded, Gnr S KENDRICK (C) wounded but remained at duty.

26 BSM WH PRESTIDGE (D) wounded but remained at duty.

30 Bdr BF VICKERY (A) shell shock.

June 1917; Major Paige; ST LEGER; HQ at T20d.7.4, Sheet 51B SW 1/20000

1   Infantry of 33rd Division relieved by Infantry of 21st Division. 100th Infantry Brigade relieved by 62nd Infantry Brigade (right sector). 98th Infantry Brigade relieved by 64th Infantry Brigade (left sector). 19th Infantry Brigade relieved by 110th Infantry Brigade (reserve).
Lt H DARE awarded Military Cross.

5   Major WT SYNNOTT awarded DSO. a/Major GEW FRANKLYN awarded Brevet Majority.

8   21st Divisional Artillery formed a barrage to support a raid by 58th Division (on right) on HINDENBURG LINE U20a.8.9 - U20b.15.45. Raid successful; one prisoner taken. *21st DA OO 67.*

9   Mentioned in dispatches: Major WT SYNNOTT (late Commanding Officer of C/94), a/Major GEW FRANKLIN, a/Capt HW COLIVER, a/Capt DS TAILYOUR, Lt AP TURNER.

14   Colonel BANISTER relinquished command of the Brigade and proceeded to England. Major D PAIGE assumed temporary command.

15   2.50am - 21st Division supported attack by 58th Division on HINDENBURG front line U20b.4.2 - U14c.3.9 by forming a Chinese Barrage. Attack successful. *21st DA OO 70.*

16   21st Division and 58th Division attack on TUNNEL TRENCH. Not successful. *21st DA OO 69.*

18-20 21st Division relieved by 33rd Division (not artillery). *21st DA OO 73.*

20-26 Bombardment of enemy defences by Corps Heavies and Field Artillery. *21st DA OO 74.*

23/24 Midnight - attack on TUNNEL TRENCH - not successful. *33rd DA OO 9.*

27	A Battery and 1 section of D Battery withdrawn for a rest.
29	8.50am - attack by 100th Infantry Brigade on TUNNEL TRENCH south of CROISILLES-FONTAINE road - not successful. *33rd DA OO 15.*
Cas	3 2/Lt R LAUCHLAN (21st TM Brigade attached to B/94) wounded but remained at duty, Dr P BEASTY (B) wounded but remained at duty. 4 Cpl C BOWDEN (D) killed, Gnr E YALLOP (D) wounded, Gnr J SENIOR (D) wounded (shell shock). 12 Gnr HR LEGARD (D) wounded. 22 Gnr RC DAVY (D) and Gnr CT CLAYTON (D) wounded. 23 Bdr T MOORE (D), Gnr RE DIXON (D) and Gnr JEM TODD (D) all wounded but remained at duty.

July 1917; Lt Col HA Boyd; HQ at T20d.7.4, Sheet 51B SW

2	Lt Col HA BOYD assumed command of the Brigade (late of 3rd Canadian Brigade).
4	A Battery returned to line from being at rest in wagon lines. D Battery withdrew to a rest camp at HENDECOURT. Guns remained in action manned by 95th Brigade.
12	Lt RW FROST (D) awarded Military Cross.
14	D Battery returned.
24	11.45pm - night raid on enemy post at U7d.52.46. Raiding party enemy on the alert and returned. *110th Infantry Brigade OO 77.*
25	2.50am - trench mortars wire cutting for a raid on MEBY at U14a 1.7 but Infantry found wire remained an obstacle. Fire by 18pdrs covered the raiding party's return. *94th Brigade OO no 47.*
Cas	16 Sgt R LAYTON (A) wounded.

August 1917; Lt AP Turner; HQ at T20d.7.4, Sheet 51B SW

13	HQ moved to T14b.4.0.
18	Raid by 1st East Yorks Regiment with objective of gaining identification. Party found wire uncut and their return covered by 18 pdr fire.
30-31	A B D Batteries relieved by 180th Brigade. *16th DA OO no 98 and 21st DA OO no 82.*
Cas	0

September 1917; Lt Col HA Boyd; BOISLEUX AU MONT

1	C Battery relieved but positions not occupied. Withdrew to wagon lines at BOISLEUX AU MONT.
1-5	At BOISLEUX AU MONT.
6-7	Entrained at ARRAS, detrained at CAESTRE. Marched to FLETRE and billeted. Map: HAZEBROUCK, 5a 1/10000.
11	Working parties to prepare positions.
12-13	Marched to RENINGHELST to relieve 106th Brigade RFA, 24th Division. A B C Batteries with A group, 190th Brigade (Col CARDEW), D Battery with Col SYMOND group under command of 41st Divisional Artillery. Brigade HQ did not go into action.
20	5.40am - attack by 124th Infantry Brigade and 122nd Infantry Brigade. (39th Division on right 23rd Division on left). Objectives gained apart from a small sector.
23	Batteries under orders of 39th Divisional Artillery along with 190th Brigade RFA.
26	Attack on objective 100 yards beyond JOIST TRENCH by 118th and 116th Infantry Brigade.
28-30	Preparation of Batteries of new positions at STIRLING

CASTLE. Map: ZILLEBEKE 6A 1/10000.

Cas 12 a/Bdr AE TWYCROSS (D), Gnr FE BOUGHEN (D), Gnr AJ BOUGHEN (D), Gnr G FORBES (D), Gnr PJ CLARKE (D), Gnr HA SAUNDERS (D), Gnr W WELLS (D), all wounded (gas). Gnr FR MASON (D) wounded (gas) but remained at duty. Gnr AJ BUTTERFIELD (C), Gnr C PEACOCK (C), Dr HJ BRIDLE (C) all wounded.

14 Gnr J WILSON (D) wounded (gas).

17 Dr JD BENNETT (A), Sgt EG NEWMAN (B), Sgt R WHITING (B), Sgt A COSTELLO (B), Gnr T MARSHALL (B) all wounded, Gnr A THOMPSON (B) killed.

19 Gnr H McKENZIE (A), Gnr H SADLER (A), Bdr JA CASWELL (C) all wounded. Gnr C BULMER (A) wounded but remained at duty.

20 a/Bdr ROBSON (A), Gnr AW POWE (B), Dr H DAVY (D) all wounded. A/Bdr D ROYLE (B) killed. Gnr P WOOD (A) accidentally injured.

21 a/Bdr D RUSSELL(C), Gnr E BLOOM (C) killed.

22 Gnr J CAMPBELL (A), Gnr A ROBERTS (A) killed. Gnr F LAMBERT (B) wounded.

23 A/Bdr H HOLMES (A), a/Bdr G AINSCOUGH (A) wounded.

24 Lt O MURRAY-LYON (D) wounded. 2Lt W BEE (D) died of wounds. Sgt HS GREENSMITH (A) wounded, Gnr HA TAYLOR (A) wounded (gas), Gnr G PRICE (B), Gnr S BALDWIN (B) both wounded but remained at duty.

25 Bdr F LIVERSEDGE (A) killed, Dr S WRIGHT (A) accidentally injured. A/Bdr B IBBOTSON (HQ) wounded.

26 Maj D PAIGE(C) wounded. Sgt AC CLARKE (B), Gnr W FAIRBROTHER (C), Gnr AG MANNING (C) all wounded but remained at duty. Gnr CH JONES (C), Gnr C MUIR (C) both killed, Gnr W CHRISTIE (C) wounded, Bdr W BRYAN (D) killed.

27 Gnr G BROWN (A) wounded (shell shock). Gnr FJ BRACE (A) wounded. Pioneer J ENGLISH (HQ), Pioneer W YOUNG (HQ) both wounded.

30 Gnr B BEARD (A) killed, Sgt W PRESCOTT (A), Gnr JH BUCKTON (A), Dr T EGAN (A), all wounded. Gnr A MARSDEN (A) wounded (gas). Dr JH BOURNE? (B), Dr WT PIKE (B), both wounded. Dr J WALKER (B) wounded but remained at duty. Gnr J WINSLADE (C),Dr A JONES (C), Dr R WILKINSON (C), Dr R WILLIAMS (C), Gnr H ARCHERS (D), Gnr J DANIEL (D), Gnr F WESTWOOD (D), Dr R CONNOLLY (D) all wounded. Gnr G THOMPSON (D) wounded (shell shock). Dr W DAWSON (D) wounded but remained at duty.

October 1917; Lt Col HA Boyd; DORMY HOUSE; HQ at I23a.5.5, Sheet No 28 NW

1-2   Completion and occupation of Battery positions at STIRLING CASTLE and SANCTUARY WOOD. Registration carried out. Brigade HQ occupied DORMY HOUSE. 94th Brigade A B C D and A and D/95 - right group commanded by Col HA Boyd.

3   6am - corps barrage.
3pm - army barrage.

4   Map: WESTHOER 1:10000. 6am - attack on line J11c.55.05 - J11d.8.5 - J11d.65.75 - J11b.95.15 - J12a.1.5. Objective gained.

5   6pm - reorganisation of artillery group. Right group (commander Lt Col HA BOYD DS0) consisted of four batteries of the 94th Brigade RFA.

6   Bdr H SWAN (B) awarded bar to Military Medal.

7   4.45am and 5.30am - corps barrage. Right group known as A group from 6pm.

8   4.45am and 5am - corps barrage. 21st Divisional Artillery became a subgroup under 7th Divisional Artillery

178

group. 21st Division withdrew and relieved by 7th Division.

9   5.20am - A group (94th Brigade) attack on REUTEL JUDGE COPSE. Most of objectives obtained.

10   4.45am - corps barrage.

11   5am - army barrage. B/94 withdrew to wagon lines. Their guns were manned by A/94.

5.10pm - corps barrage.

12   5.15am - artillery barrage. 2nd ANZAC corps attacked PASSHENDALE. 7th Divisional Artillery group cooperated by forming a barrage in depth with a view of simulating an attack on BECELAERE.

10am - reorganisation of artillery groups 94th Brigade (Group A) with B+D/315 commanded by Lt Col HA BOYD.

13   5.15am - army barrage.

14   B/94 returned to line. A/94 withdrew to wagon lines.

15   Cpl RJ OLDS (A) awarded Military Medal.

18   Dr G MANSHIP (B), Gnr T WARD (B), Pnr J ENGLISH (HQ) awarded Military Medal.

19   HQ of 94th Brigade withdrew. Lt Col TA HIGGINBOTHAM DSO resumed command of A group and took over HQ at DORMY HOUSE.

24   12pm - 94th Brigade returned to line. Lt Col HA BOYD resumed command. Capt RHAS GEDDES (C) and 2/Lt F MARSHALL (B) awarded Military Cross. Sgt EC STOKOE (A) awarded Dist. Conduct Medal. Cpl AV METCALF (A), Sgt B SLACK (A), Ftr T MOBBS (A), Bdr R NEWMAN (A) all awarded Military Medal.

26   5.40am - 7th Division attacked GHELUVELT and 5th Division attacked POLDERHOER CHATEAU and WOOD. A group carried out task allocated by 5th Divisional Artillery - searching square J17a. Later switched to defensive line. 5th Division took POLDERHOER CHATEAU but lost it later that night.

29   5.15am - army barrage.
      Maj RJ WEIL (A) and 2 Lt C NORMAN (A) awarded Military
      Cross. Gnr E GIBBARD (D) awarded Military Medal.

30   5.30am - Canadian corps on left attacked
      PASSCHENDALE. A group covered 21st Divisional Infantry
      and took part in task of X corps (to simulate an attack
      on GHELUVELT and BECELAERE).

31   5.15am - corps barrage. Other barrages carried out
      following orders received by telephone.
      During the two months there was barrage lasting 30
      mins between 5am and 6am each day. Positions at
      STIRLING CASTLE were heavily shelled by the enemy
      throughout the month, particularly during practice
      barrages which lasted over half an hour and to which the
      enemy usually replied by shelling the area. Started with
      nine 18 pdr Batteries from 94th, 95th and 190th Brigades.
      By 10.10.17 only 6 Batteries remained. (190th Brigade
      had withdrawn). By the end of the month one Battery
      of 94th Brigade manning three remaining guns that had
      originally belonged to five most southerly Batteries.
      Getting ammunition to guns was difficult and led to a
      good many casualties at start of month but owing to the
      large numbers of guns put out of action, of which the
      ammunition dumps were available for the remainder, it
      was seldom found necessary to replenish ammunition
      later on.

Cas   1 Dr P HARTSHORN (A) and Bdr R HEATON (D)
      wounded.
      2 Capt JE MULLER (C) wounded. 2Lt EM PEARCE (C)
      wounded but remained at duty. Sgt JA GARNER (A), Sgt
      C HOPTON (B), Sgt AC CLARKE (B), Gnr H GOLDIE (C),
      Gnr SD GEDDIS (C), Gnr J COCKS (C), Gnr G WOOD (D)
      all wounded.
      3 Gnr G WOODING (A) killed. Sgt SC STOKOE (A), Cpl
      T PARNABY (A), Gnr G DAVIDSON (A), Gnr H GENT (A),

Gnr JE STEWART (A) all wounded (gas). Gnr A WILSON (A), Gnr S KEENAN (A) wounded (gas), both attached to TM Bde and Dr GILBERT (HQ) killed.

4 Lt J SCOTT (B) wounded. BSM FE BIRD (A) killed. Cpl WG STAGGS (A), Bdr B ASPDEN (A), Gnr R LISLE (A), Gnr G GOODLIFFE (A) all wounded. Gnr RW GUNMAN (A), Gnr SJ SHELLARD (A), Gnr F PENFOLD (A), Dr WC BRUCE (A) all killed. Gnr D LANGFORD (B), Sgt TJ BRETON (B), Gnr F HOGG (B), Gnr B KELLY (B), Gnr H LOCKHEART (B), Gnr AJ CUMMINGS? (B), Bdr G HALL (B), Dr J WALKER (B) all wounded. Bdr G MORTIMER (B), Gnr FD CLEGG (B), Gnr GILDERT (B - attached to TM) all killed. Gnr N MUNRO (C), Gnr D LE ROY (C) wounded. Bdr JM MANN (C), Dr E WEEDON (C), Dr E PLOWRIGHT (C), Dr J ELLIS (C) all wounded but remained at duty. Bdr CJ SHARP (C) killed. Bdr CJ DAVIS (D), Gnr E YARDLEY (D), Gnr R THOMPSON (D) all killed.

5 Bdr W DUNN (B) wounded.

6 Sgt JA HODGKISS (B), Cpl J LAWRENCE (B), Cpl J HOPPER (C), Gnr H SMITH (D) all wounded. Cpl J KNOTT (C) killed.

7 Sgt E BLACKBURN (A) wounded, a/Bdr A WHALLEY (A) wounded but remained at duty. Gnr S MARTIN (B), Dr FL ARMSTRONG (B), Dr H RHODES (B), Dr H BROWN (B), Gnr EVANS (C), Gnr ROBINSON (C), Gnr F FLOWER (D), Gnr BEILBY (D) all wounded. Gnr M LOCKHEAD (C) missing since 4 October.

8 Cpl A GAMAGE (C), a/Bdr TJ EDWARDS (C), Bdr A GORDON (C), Gnr G ALLAN (C), Gnr J GILROY (C), Dr W BEAL (C) all wounded. Dr S VOYCE (C) killed.

9 Lt CP CAMPBELL (B) wounded, since died of wounds. S Sgt Ftn W POOLE (A), a/Bdr JS JACKSON (A), Gnr R WILLIAMS (A), Gnr AA LLOYD (A), Sgt RJ DOBBINS (B), Ftr CH BRAGG (B), Gnr W GREEN (B), Gnr WW FISH (D) all wounded.

10 Lt RW FROST (D) killed. 2Lt TM HUME (A) wounded (gas) but remained at duty. Cpl H METCALF (A) wounded. Bdr W BLANT (A) wounded (gas). Gnr H FLETCHER (A) wounded (shell shock). Gnr J CHRISTIAN (A), Dr A STEWART (C) wounded but remained at duty. Bdr JY BRABBINGS (B), Dr R BELL (C), Bdr W THOMPSON (D), Gnr W JONES (D), Gnr G MITCHELL (D), Dr J HARWOOD (D), Dr R KEYMER (D) all wounded. Dr H THOMPSON (C) killed.

11 Dr P McNAMARA (A) killed. Gnr A SMITH (D), Gnr CF RYE (D) wounded.

14 Dr J BERTRAM (A) wounded. Gnr CR EUGACE (D), Gnr GC POPE (D) killed.

15 Gnr G FLOWER (C) wounded but remained at duty. Gnr A STELL (C), Gnr AH GOODWIN (D) wounded. Cpl QS(TS?) BAYLIS (D), Gnr AG COPLEY (D), Gnr BOA (D) all wounded (gas).

16 Cap DS TAILYOUR (B), 2Lt CALDER (B) wounded (gas) - both returned after 4 days in hospital. 2Lt EB REID (B) wounded (gas). Gnr HW CLARKE (B), Gnr W QUIRIE (B) wounded (gas).

17 Gnr E GIBBERD (D), Gnr AH PAYNE (D) wounded (gas).

18 2Lt GC HEWITT (D) wounded (gas). Gnr D COOK (B), Gnr F FORSYTH (B) wounded (gas).

19 Gnr NH SIMPSON (A), Gnr J SYGROVE (A), Gnr LAWSON (A), Gnr G KIRKBRIDGE (A), Gnr C PARKER (A) all wounded (gas).

21 Cpl T HENRY (A), Bdr JW EDWARDS (A) wounded (gas). a/Bdr G CARLIN (A) injured.

23 Dr HL DUNKERTON (D) wounded.

24 Cpl M PARKINSON (A), a/Bdr W ATKINSON (A), Gnr L WARD (A), Gnr J DARWIN (A), Gnr PE DIXON (D), Gnr PF RAWLE (D), Gnr JEM TODD (D), Gnr G WILKINSON

(D), Gnr HURLE (D - attached from TM Brigade) all wounded (gas).

25 Sgt B SLACK (A), Dr J ESKDALE (A), Cpl J CAMPBELL (A attached from TM Brigade) all wounded (gas). Bdr J RUMNEY (B) missing. Gnr GILL, Gnr MARSHALL, Gnr VOYCE (all D but attached from TM Brigade) wounded. Gnr GIRLING (D but attached from TM Brigade) wounded but remained at duty.

26 Sgt HW RANDELL (B), Bdr THACKERY (B), Gnr S KINGHAM (B), Gnr WO CLARKE (B), Gnr ROYSTON (B) all wounded.

29 Sgt RJ OLDS (A), Bdr CR KINDALL (A), Gnr C BULMER (A), Gnr HMB SMITH (A), Gnr G SMITH (A), Gnr J BRADSHAW (A), Gnr J ROGERS (A), Gnr JJ JACKSON (A), Ftr T MOBBS (A), Gnr F DYSON (A), Sgt JS HOUSE (C), Bdr JG DUCKETT (C), Gnr AD JOHNSON (C), Gnr ROWE (C), Gnr H HOWARD (C), Gnr W McINTOCH (C) all wounded (gas). Gnr M DOBSON (C) wounded.

30 2/Lt JE HARDING (D) killed. Maj AQ ARCHDALE (C), 2Lt GG McFARLANE (C), 2/Lt JH PERROTT (C) all wounded (gas). Sgt GH SHERWIN (B), Bdr BURKE (B), Gnr AB COLES (B), Gnr JT ADAMS (B), Gnr HC JACOBS (B), Dr P KENNEDY (B), Cpl J MURRY (C), Cpl A HEATHERTON (C), Gnr H HARROWER (C), Gnr AR PURCELL (C) all wounded (gas). Bdr JE OAKLEY (D) killed. Gnr HR LEGARD (D) wounded.

31 Gnr W ADAM (A), Gnr H GIBBONS (C), Gnr WC KING (C), Dr D GODSALL (C), Dr J GIBSON (C), all wounded (gas). Bdr FH PRIME (D), Gnr J OSBORNE (D) wounded.

November 1917; Lt Col HA Boyd; DORMY HOUSE; Sheet No 28 NW 1/20000

1   5.15am - corps barrage. *21st DA Inst 12.*

4   5.45am - corps barrage. *21st DA Inst 13.*

5   4.50am - corps barrage. *21st DA Inst 13.*
     4/5 - gas shell bombardment by D/94 and D/95 on J18a.9.0 - J18b.7.7 in preparation for attack.

6   6am - creeping barrage for attack by 5th Division attack on POLDERHOEK CHATEAU. (Eighteen 18pdrs involved from 94th and 95th Brigade. Batteries - A/94, C/95 and B/94). Line from J16c.7.0 - J16d.0.2 *21st DA instr no 16.* D/94 and D/95 simulated an attack of BECELAERE with howitzers. Smoke and gas shells on a line J18c.5.7 - J12c.8.0. Attack not successful.

7   5.30am - army barrage. *21st DA instr no 17.*

8/9   C/94 and C/95 relieved 7th Divisional Artillery after resting in wagon lines.

9   A group now became right group (94th and 95th Brigades). *21st DA OO no 89.*

13   Right group relieved by 14th Army Brigade RFA and 39th Divisional Artillery. *21st DA OO no 90.* Positions reorganised into 4 gun and 2 gun positions. Much labour needed to move guns. Brigade concentrated in wagon lines at RENINGHELST.

15   Map: HAZEBROUCK, 5a 1/10000. Marched to MORBECQUE and billeted for the night. *21st DA OO no 92.*

17   Brigade marched to VENDIN LES BETHUNE and billeted. *21st DA OO no 93.*

18   Brigade marched to HOUDAIN.

19   Brigade marched to ESTREE COUCHE. *21st DA OO no 94.* Map: LENS 11.

20/22   21st Divisional Artillery relieved 47th Division. B/94 and D/94 relieved B/236 and D/236. *21st DA OO no 95.*

22	HQ and A and C Batteries marched to rest billets at CAPELLE FERMONT and FREVIN CAPELLE. Brigade HQ at FREVIN CAPELLE.
24	B and D Batteries relieved by C/170 and D/170 and withdrew to wagon lines.
26	B and D/94 marched to rest billets at BERLE and VANDELICOURT.
30	3.30pm - verbal orders for all Batteries to march to ARRAS. All left by 5.45pm. Bivouaced near ARRAS - ST POL Road. HQ at VICTORY CAMP. Destination not given. *21st DA OO no 99.*
Cas	1 Gnr S JACKSON (B), Cpl SB PECK (D), Gnr J FRANGLETON (D) all gassed. Gnr R HOOD (C) gassed but now at duty.

2 Gnr A McLENNAN (A), Sgt TR TAPLIN (B), Gnr W FAIRBROTHER (C), Gnr T MULLIS (D) all gassed.

3. Sgt LW LISTER (D), Cpl MUGGLESTON (D), Gnr E DYE (D) all gassed. Sgt A SMITH (AVC) found dead in bivouac.

4. Gnr W RILEY (A), Gnr AL RUSSELL (A), Sgt C DAVIS (C), Gnr J RAMSEY (D), all gassed.

5. Gnr A LOFTHOUSE (C), Gnr P TRAYNOR (C), Gnr WG SIMPSON (C), Gnr J GROOMBRIDGE (C), Gnr LD HOPE (D) all gassed. Gnr R FARLEY (C) gassed but at duty.

6. Gnr H BLEACKLEY (B), Gnr R ROBINSON (C), Gnr J SMITH (C), Gnr W THOMPSON (C). Bdr JM MANN (C), Gnr JA ROBINSON (C), Sgt CW NOTTINGHAM (C), Sgt GW YENSON (D), all gassed.

7. Gnr W TURDDY (B), Gnr R WILLIAMSON (D) gassed.

8. Gnr O GRAY (A), Gnr J STOCKDALE (A), Gnr O THOMAS (A), a/Bdr J ROBERTS (B), Gnr MD MUNRO (C), Gnr WC KING (C), Gnr W DURRANT (D), Gnr GW SENIOR (D), Gnr F DOWNEY (D), all gassed. a/Bdr TJ SMITH (C) gassed but remained at duty. Bdr F TILL (B) wounded now at duty.

24 a/Bdr E TURNER (C) wounded.

December 1917; Major STANKLYN?; ST QUENTIN

1   March to BEAULENCOURT near BAPAUME. Bivouacs in field. Weather very cold and insufficient tents provided. *DA OO 100.*

2   Marched to BRUSLE. Bivouac - covered standing for horses and Nissen huts for personnel. *21st DA OO 101.*

3-4   Brigade marched into wagon lines at K5c.8.3 on ROISEL - STE EMILIE road. Positions selected and dug south of EPEHY. Brigade HQ at STE EMILIE E24b.3.7 (Sheet 57C SE). All Batteries into action and covered right Brigade (110th Infantry Brigade) which had taken over the line between MALASSISE FARM and CATALET ROAD. Battery positions: A F13a.77.20, B F13a.73.85, C E12d.99.10, D F13a.38.37. Order of Batteries from right to left A B C with D superimposed over whole front. *21st DA OO 103.*

5   OP in EPEHY (F1b.2.2) occupied with Infantry.

11   Forward guns provided by A and B Batteries (one gun each) placed in a semi-covered position in EPEHY (F1b.15.40) to fire with open sights in the event of the enemy breaking through down THRUSH and CATALET VALLEYS. Capt HW COLLIVER, Lt T SCOTT, Ftr H BAMFORD mentioned in dispatches.

13   6.30pm - test of SOS rockets. Nothing observed owing to fog.

19   Further test of SOS signal. Failure due to fog.

21/22 Harassing fire of entire brigade zone throughout the night. 100 rounds per Battery of ammunition allotted. *21st DA OO 109.*

26   Position of A and D 275th AFA Brigade RFA taken over at E12a.9.3 and E12b.30.16.

27   To occupy these positions guns transferred by Batteries as follows A 1, B 1, C 2, D 2. Wagon lines transferred to SAULCOURT.

Cas   10 2/Lt C SMITH wounded.
      21 Gnr H DRANE wounded.
      28 Gnr R STRIKE wounded but remained at duty.

Chapter 7
1918 - The Spring Offensive

Winter 1918

The winter of 1917-1918 was cold. The Allies were still waiting for American troops to arrive in large numbers but the war against the U-Boats in the Atlantic had been largely won and supplies were usually getting through. On the other hand, the Russian Revolution resulted in an ending of hostilities on the Eastern Front and Germany could now devote 44 extra divisions to France and Belgium.[1] However the hardships suffered by German civilians in 1917 were worsening; riots and strikes were becoming common and martial law was declared in Hamburg and Brandenburg.[2] In Britain food shortages had resulted in increased prices; the cost of some products such as bread, potatoes, dairy products and meat had doubled. As a result some voluntary food rationing schemes had been implemented to reduce consumption. Such voluntary schemes were strengthened in some areas by local compulsory rationing and in February 1918 general food rationing was introduced over the whole country for certain goods, for example sugar, butter, and later, meat.[3]

Jack and his brigade were still in France near Epéhy and as usual for the winter months, no offensives were taking place. Indeed the 94th Brigade's War Diary does not mention any barrages or other shooting until 13th March.

There is a different feel in the diary though; it is as if the brigade is waiting for something to happen. There are many descriptions of preparations for an enemy attack; guns were calibrated, there were long "silent periods" and SOS signals were tested.

There were other more specific preparations, for example

> *17ᵗʰ January 1918 - 2.00am - message received saying enemy message had been picked up "Be ready 4.00am". All Batteries warned to be keenly on alert.*

> *27ᵗʰ February 1918 - 4.45pm - as a test of a scheme for reinforcing the front in case of attack, Brigade ordered to move into action immediately. DRIENCOURT cleared by 5.30pm. Rendezvous reached by 6.30pm.⁴*

In order to find out more, raids on enemy trenches took place for example on 16ᵗʰ March and later (recorded in the 21ˢᵗ Division General Staff HQ Diary) on 19ᵗʰ March:

> *Successful raid on BEET TRENCH. 5 prisoners taken. From prisoners' statements it appears that hostile attack may take place 20ᵗʰ/21ˢᵗ or 21ˢᵗ/22ⁿᵈ March.⁵*

The same diary also records that on 20ᵗʰ March:

> *A heavy ground mist continued for most of the day but towards end of the day the mist lifted for a short period, during which considerable movement was seen in German lines.⁶*

Despite these preparations, the brigade was not up to full strength; on 13ᵗʰ-14ᵗʰ March, 'B' Battery was selected for training and left the area for 5ᵗʰ Army Artillery School. They stayed away until 26ᵗʰ March.

It was during this time, on 17ᵗʰ January, that Jack wrote his last two surviving letters home, to his sisters Ana and Gladys. As usual in his letters he does not talk much of his own situation, although he does refer to the weather and his health:

The weather has broken here now and oh there's not half some mud about. We are having much rain which makes it seem like home.[7]

I've had a bad cold for a day or two but I am getting rid of it now, and am getting quite well again.[8]

Perhaps due to the cold, the Senior Supply Officer seems especially concerned with ensuring the 21st Division had a good supply of fruit and vegetables; on 29th January and 28th February oranges were acquired, although only enough for about half an orange per man. He also mentions cabbage and carrots, although these seem to have been provided mainly for horses.[9]

March 21st 1918

The officers of Jack's division were right to think that a German offensive was coming but were not prepared for the power of the attack. General Ludendorff, the German Commander, knew that his 192 divisions on the Western Front were numerically superior to the Allies who had 173 divisions, many of which were seriously weakened by the long conflict - on average British divisions were about 2,000 men under strength.[10] He also knew that American troops would start arriving in large numbers by the summer and that the spring of 1918 was therefore the last chance for Germany to win the war. He had planned a strategy with the aim of smashing through the Allied front lines and pushing them back as far as possible, hopefully to the Channel ports.

Ludendorff's tactics were not new. He planned to start with a massive artillery bombardment and 6,473 guns were deployed able to fire about 1,160,000 shells.[11] These would destroy communications (even telephone wires buried six feet deep) and headquarters behind the lines and send gas and high explosives into the British front lines. After this, "storm troops"

- highly mobile units equipped with weapons such as flame throwers, machine guns and grenades would aim to destroy allied defences. Later, the infantry would move through the gaps in the lines and occupy the ground gained.

It would still have been dark at 4.40am on 21st March when the German artillery bombardment started.[12] The weather was foggy which added confusion to the situation in the British lines around St. Quentin which was where Ludendorff had chosen to begin the assault which he knew as the Kaiserschlacht (Kaiser's Battle).

The bombardment lasted for five hours and had a overwhelming effect on British troops in the opposite lines. Lieutenant William Carr, 377 Battery RFA, described it as follows:

> Think of the loudest clap of thunder you have ever heard then imagine what it would be like if it continued without stopping. That was the noise which woke us at 4.40am on Thursday 21st March. I have never before or since heard anything like it.[13]

At 9.40am the next phase of the attack began and German troops started attacking the front lines; it did not take long for these to be taken. As Martin Middlebrook says:

> Within less than an hour of the commencement of the German Infantry attack, the British front line had disappeared for fifty miles ... except for a few isolated posts still holding out but so scattered and weak as to be of no further significance.[14]

Many trenches had been abandoned quickly, sometimes even before the storm troops had arrived and the British retreated to reserve defences. These soon began to fall too and by noon, only 15 positions in the battle zone around St. Quentin (held by the British Fifth Army) were still in British hands. Two of these, near Vaucelette Farm and Epéhy were being defended by men of the 21st Division, supported by artillery fire from brigades such as the 94th. Indeed the writer of the 21st Division General Staff HQ Diary, when summarising the events of the morning wrote:

> *The enemy were undoubtedly held off on this flank for a considerable period by the action of the Batteries of the 94th Brigade RFA who continued firing at the enemy at point blank range up till the last possible moment.*[15]

Fighting continued through the afternoon with the Germans taking more ground in many places. Vaucelette Farm fell in mid afternoon but Epéhy held out. According to the 21st Division General Staff HQ Diary this was because the morale of the troops was high, they had good officers, work put in on the trenches (for example wire and good digging) was effective and the fact that machine guns were well-sighted.

The batteries of the 94th Brigade moved back in the afternoon to previously prepared positions. 'A' Battery had to abandon all but one of its guns; the others were captured by the enemy.

By the time that night fell at 7.50pm, the Germans had captured over 98½ square miles of land which had been occupied by the British at daybreak. This was as much land as the Allies had gained in the 140 days of the Battle of the Somme in 1916.[16] Due to the confused nature of the battle it is hard to be precise about casualty figures for the day but Martin Middlebrook gives the following estimates:

German Army
10,851 killed
28,778 wounded
300 prisoners
Total - 39,929 casualties

British Army
7,512 killed
10,000 wounded
21,000 prisoners
Total - 38,512 casualties[17]

These combined figures represent the highest casualty rates for any single day in the Great War. One of these casualties was Jack. Sadly, at the age of 22, after surviving the horrors of the Somme and Passchendaele without injury for three and a half years and after travelling over 750 miles around northern France and Belgium, his luck had run out.

On 21st March it was not certain that he had actually been killed and the 94th Brigade's War Diary simply states:

Bdr J W GARBUTT (C) wounded and missing.

Sometime later a letter - telegrams were usually only sent to the families of officers - arrived at Chop Gate Post Office and the postman trudged up the hill to Wingroves to deliver the news that Isaac and Mary Emma had been dreading. The arrival of this news might have taken three weeks or more given the difficulties with communications at the time.

The letter received by the Garbutts is no longer in existence, but it would have contained army form B.104-83 which was used to give notification of missing men:

I regret to have to inform you that a report has been received from the War Office to the effect that _____ was reported as missing on _____

The form went on to say that this did not mean the soldier was dead and it could be a year or two before form 82A was sent to tell the family that:

It is my painful duty to inform you that no further news having been received relative to _____ the Army Council have regretfully constrained to conclude that he is dead.[18]

The first letter clearly left some doubt for the family and on 8th May 1918, his sister Gladys wrote to France asking for more details of the events of 21st March. She received the following reply:

22nd May 1918

Dear Miss Garbutt

The Commanding Officer has handed me your letter of the 8th May and requested me to reply thereto as I am the only officer who knows the circumstances relating to your Brother.

On the 21st March last, I was in charge of 6 ammunition wagons drawing ammunition urgently needed at the guns. Your Brother and another Bombardier were my NCOs. The roads were being heavily shelled at the time but we had orders to get through. All went well until [we were] close to some crossroads, when some heavy calibre shells burst quite close. One of the drivers and two of the horses of the leading team were wounded and my horse was badly wounded also. I got the leading wagon out of the way and ordered the remaining wagons to proceed. I then shot my horse and caught, after some difficulty, one that was riderless. I gave orders to the drivers of the wounded team and then rode on and caught up [with] the remainder.

When we got to a sunken point of the road, more or less under cover, I ascertained that both my NCOs were missing. I assumed that your Brother had fallen from his horse and would in due course, report at the wagon lines. At the time the pace was a fast as possible and he would not have been able to catch us up.

We eventually got up the ammunition and returned to the wagon lines. Altogether there were four casualties to men but all were accounted for, except your Brother.

Every enquiry has been made that is possible to locate him, but without success.

The place in question soon fell into enemy hands and if he was hit and survived, the Enemy would have, no doubt, informed our Government through the usual channels. As up to now the division has heard nothing. I fear, (and with this the commanding officer agrees), that he must have been killed.

The Battery has missed him very much. He was good at his duties, respected by his officers and liked by all the men.

I am desired by the Major and brother Officers to convey to you and your family, our deepest sympathy,

Yours faithfully

Frank W Pearse
2/Lt

Jack's great adventure was at an end.

Letters 1918

1. Letter from Jack to Diana [January 17ᵗʰ 1918]

Dear Sister Ana

  just a few lines in answer of your ever welcome letter which I recieved safely on the 12ᵗʰ of Jan. So pleased to hear you were quite well. I recieved your Photo safely. I think it is very much like you. The weather as broken here now and oh theys not half some mud about. We are having much rain which makes it *[illegible]*. Pleased to hear you had a good Xmas and how well you seem to like Newlands. I am writing Bob a few lines too. He will get a letter about the same time as you. Well Ana, I haven't got much to tell you this time so will draw to a close hoping you are all well at Newlands as it leaves me in the best of health with love and all best wishes from your affec Brother
     J W Garbutt

2. Letter from Jack to Gladys [January 17ᵗʰ 1918]

My Dear Sister Gladys

  I now take pleasure in answering your last and ever welcome letter and Card which I recieved safely on the 9ᵗʰ of Jan. So pleased to hear you were quite well. I've had a bad cold for a day or two but I am getting rid of it now, and am getting quite well again. Leave that to me. Gladys I shall say nothing of what you have told me If Ana as said anything to darken your life she might be sorry for it some day when she get to know better She is young and silly yet but she will get to know things better when she gets older. Well Gladys I haven't got much time so will ring off with love and best wishes from Your loving Brother
     J.W. Garbutt
       Bon Soir
         write Soon

94th Brigade RFA, War Diary
January-March 1918
January 1918; Lt Col HA Boyd;
STE EMILIE; HQ at E24b.3.7, sheet 62C NE

1	SOS lines of C/95 taken over at X20d.2.1 - X20c.90.35.
4	Lt BB EDGE joined from J/RHA; posted to D Battery.
6	Major CM TAYLOR (D) awarded Military Cross. Sgt EG NEWMAN (B) awarded DCM.
10	Capt JE MULLER rejoined the Brigade - wounded at Ypres. Posted to B Battery.
12	SOS lines of C Battery altered to X20c.35.70 - X20a.0.0.
15	7.30-9.15pm - raiding party to enemy position at X26b.95.50 covered by A and B Batteries who stood to, to engage three machine guns in case of difficulty.
17	2am - message received saying enemy message had been picked up "Be ready 4am". All Batteries warned to be keenly on alert.
	4am - enemy raided HEYTHORT POST (north of LEMPIRE) on our right. 5 men of Queen's regiment taken prisoner.
20	Silent period for 24 hours from 8am. No use of telephones allowed.
23	Silent period as above. SOS signal changed to 2 red and 2 green lights.
25	Support for a raid by 62nd Infantry Brigade planned but this postponed and then cancelled.
27	Capt AH HORNBY posted to Brigade; with B Battery in place of Capt MULLER who was evacuated.
29	8pm - test of SOS signals. All rockets but one were seen but indistinct. Unfavourable reports 2/Lts BARTLETT, WEBSTER and MELLOW posted to A, B and C Batteries respectively.
Cas	0

February 1918; Lt Col HA Boyd; STE EMILIE; HQ at E24b.3.7, sheet 62C NE

1   Silent period 8am-8pm.

2   Brigade less C Battery relieved by A B D/95th. Withdrew to wagon lines at SAULCOURT for training. *DA Order No 6.*

5   B Battery calibrated guns at range at LE QUINCONCEL (sheet 62C, I21).

11   B Battery relieved C Battery who went to wagon lines at SAULCOURT.

12   HQ and wagon lines of C and D Batteries moved to DRIENCOURT lately occupied by No 2 and 3 sections of 21st DAC. (Sheet 62C, J3d). A Battery calibrated guns at range at LE QUINCONCEL.

13   A Battery moved wagon lines to DRIENCOURT.

14   C Battery calibrated guns.

16   D Battery calibrated guns.

17   6.30pm - extensive enemy air raid until midnight around TEMPLEUX LA FOSSE, DRIENCOURT, TINCOURT and BUSSU. 250 - 300 bombs dropped. Sheet 62C NE.

19   A Battery occupied new wagon lines at LONGAVESNES and in evening returned to line to relieve B Battery who withdrew from their gun positions and wagon lines back to DRIENCOURT for further training.

27   4.45pm - as a test of a scheme for reinforcing the front in case of attack, Brigade ordered to move into action immediately. DRIENCOURT cleared by 5.30pm. Rendezvous (E27 central) reached by 6.30pm. Brigade under command of 16th Division.

7.10pm - ordered to occupy their late positions in the line.

7.25pm - started off via VILLERS FAUCHON and reached positions and ready to fire on SOS lines by 8.15pm. Then returned to DRIENCOURT.

28   Brigade moved at short notice to new wagon lines at LONGAVESNES. DRIENCOURT cleared by 4.30pm. Went into action on same evening in support of 110th Infantry Brigade. B Battery new position at E17a.6.0. C and D Batteries returned to those they had previously occupied, except D Battery put their detached section in B Batteries late main position instead of "D.X" as formerly. Sgt W DAVIS (D) and Bdr G OWENS (C) awarded Croix de Guerre (Belgium).

Cas   19 Cpl A HALLAM (B) wounded in action GSW.

March 1918; Lt Col HA Boyd; STE EMILIE

13   Artillery support was given by D Battery to a successful raid carried out by 2nd Royal Munster Fusiliers (16th Divisional Artillery) at midnight 13th/14th.

13/14   B Battery having been selected as training Battery for 5th Army Artillery School were relieved in the line by C/95th Brigade RFA. They withdrew to their wagon lines at LONGAVESNES overnight and commenced their six days at 9am on 14.3.18.

16   11.30pm - all Batteries gave the protection of their fire to a party of the 6th Batallion Leicester Regiment (21st Division) who carried out a successful raid on enemy trenches about sheet 62C NE, X21b. Prisoners were captured and the rest of the garrison killed without casualty to our men who were back in their trenches by midnight.

21   4.30-4.45am - the preparatory bombardment of the great German Offensive began. Owing to the 16th Division on our right being forced back and our encirclement thereby being threatened, Batteries were withdrawn during the afternoon to previously selected positions at SAULCOURT. HQ was transferred to SAULCOURT -

LONGAVESNES road. A Battery were only able to get one gun away, the remainder falling into the hands of the enemy.

22 11am - orders received to withdraw to BROWN LINE with a switch from SAULCOURT to TINCOURT WOOD to protect our right flank. The Brigade withdrew at once to positions just north of AIZECOURT LE BAS in accordance with the 21st Divisional Artillery orders.

5pm - half of the Batteries retired by order of 21st Divisional Artillery to previously selected positions for defence of GREEN LINE at north east end of BUSSU WOOD. The remainder were to retire at 8pm, but owing to the speedy advance of the enemy, C/94 whose teams were up, was forced to take up intermediate positions at north end of EPINETTE WOOD and from there engaged the enemy at west edge of LIERAMONT. As teams were not up, 3 Howitzers belonging to D/94 had to be abandoned. Sights and Breech Blocks were removed.

8pm - the remainder of C/94 retired and rejoined the Battery near BUSSU WOOD.

23 HQ at BUSSU. 8am - orders received to withdraw and take up new positions west of PERONNE-BOUCHAVESNES road. At the request of the GOC 64th Infantry Brigade, Batteries remained in action until 9.15am to cover retirement of infantry from GREEN LINE. Fresh positions were taken up just behind MOUNT ST QUENTIN and all Batteries were in action again by 11am. Up to noon, no enemy were in sight from forward OPs so likely places of assembly west of DRIENCOURT were fired on. Just after noon the advancing enemy came into view and were engaged continually until 3pm when a further retirement became necessary owing to the presence of the enemy in PERONNE and the fact that MOUNT ST QUENTIN could not be cleared at short range. Orders had been received from the 21st Divisional Artillery at 2.30pm that the next line of resistance would be CLERY-BOUCHAVESNES

and gun positions on the line HEM-MAUREPAS. The retirement of the Brigade was commenced about 3pm. Roads were very congested, progress being reduced to not more that 1 mile per hour and enemy aircraft became very active with machine guns but with remarkably little effect. Batteries dropped into action just west of HALLE (I13a) to engage, at short range, enemy infantry advancing from HAUT ALLAINES. Very effective shooting was done through good observation within voice control of Batteries. Batteries withdrew further in the evening and got into action north east of GURLU by midnight. On this day three guns under Lt CHAPMAN, who was unable to ascertain the situation, were coming up via PERONNE to replace casualties in the A/94th. When near PERONNE it was discovered that our own infantry had retired and line of enemy infantry were advancing in full view. Lt CHAPMAN at once brought his gun into action with open sights firing all the ammunition in gun limbers, doing considerable execution, and got guns away without mishap. He rejoined his Battery during the night.

24   During the day, 3 Howitzers joined D Battery making the strength of the Brigade up to the following: A/94 4 guns, C/94 5 guns, D/94 6 Howitzers. B Battery had not yet rejoined from the 5th Army artillery school. Owing to poor visibility the enemy did not come into view until 9am.

9am-noon - infantry continued to retire steadily and the enemy were continually engaged by all guns of the Brigade.

About noon - Brigade retired by order of 21st Divisional Artillery to positions about A24c and subsequently to A22. At about 6.30pm our infantry (now 35th Division) were holding a line about 1000 yards east of MARICOURT and the Brigade was withdrawn to positions about B20c under 35th Divisional Artillery orders.

25 Brigade remained in action all day covering infantry line east of MARICOURT. This line although heavily attacked was maintained south and east of village but driven back somewhat north of it.

8pm – orders for retirement were received and the Brigade moved about 10.00pm to E23 marching via SUZANNE and BRAY road. A Battery remained in action until 2am and maintained an increasingly rapid rate of fire so as to hide the withdrawal of other Batteries. Prior to this retirement A/95, D/95 and C/94 were withdrawn from the line, handing over their guns to the remaining Batteries of 21st Divisional Artillery which came under HQ 94th Brigade RFA. HQ 95th Brigade RFA were withdrawn from the line.

26 5.30am - Batteries were in action, 18 pdrs in K23c and D/94 in quarry about K29 central covering line running north from BRAY.

8am - orders were received to move across the ANCRE and take up positions to cover the crossing at TREUX. Batteries were all in action by 2am, 18 pdrs in D10c and 4.5 Howitzers in D17c. On this day B/94 rejoined the Brigade from 5th Army Artillery school and came into action in D16d. HQ was established at D9 central (apx). Further retirement was checked from this date as our Infantry succeeded in holding the line of the railway between DERNANCOURT and BUIRE. Visibility greatly improved from this date and on subsequent days. Batteries had most successful shoots on concentrations of the enemy with good observations.

29 A/94 and D/94 and HQ 94th Brigade were relieved by the corresponding units of the 95th Brigade and withdrew to BAIZIEUX.

30 C/94 was relieved in the line by C/95 and withdrew to BEAUCOURT to which place the rest of the 94th Brigade (less B/94 who still remained in action) had proceeded earlier in the day.

Cas 21 2/Lt CJ NORMAN (A), Bdr R GREEN (A), Gnr R YOUNG (A), Gnr D PATTERSON (A), Gnr JA HOWARD (A), Gnr GW CREASEY (A), Gnr D GRIGGS (A) wounded. Gnr D LESLIE (A) missing. **Bdr JW GARBUTT (C) wounded and missing.** Dr FW TREATH (C), Gnr GW LAMB (C), Gnr R HOOD (C) wounded Gnr G DRYSDALE (C) Dr F LAWLER (C) wounded (gas). Lt BB EDGE (D), 2/Lt FA RUSTON (D), Gnr J KEAT (D), Gnr E WALLBANK (D), Gnr J BALL (D) wounded. L/Bdr R OAKLEY (D) killed in action. Gnr WH WILSON (D) died of wounds. Lpr JA MILES (HQ) wounded.

22 Dr A DOMMIE (A) killed in action. Dr T TRICE (A), Dr EC MARTIN (A) wounded. Bdr G OWEN (C), Gnr J GORMLEY (C), Gnr H LEIGHTON (C) wounded. Gnr A MANNING (C) wounded but at duty. Dr J TRILL (HQ),Dr A CUTTER (HQ) wounded. Capt BJ MULLIN (RAMC) wounded.

23 Gnr A TELEY (A) missing. Cpl H TRILTON (A) wounded. 2/Lt NH BURFITT (A) wounded but at duty.

27 Sgt E BLACKBURN (A), Gnr W ANDERSON (A) wounded. Gnr F KEELEY (A), Gnr W TURNBULL (A), Gnr H GRAY (A) killed in action. Dr J TIERNEY (D) wounded but at duty.

28 Pnr W WEBB (HQ) died of wounds.

29 2/Lt EMV SPAULL (B) killed in action. Dr N CUBB (B), and Dr W TALBUT (B) wounded.

Chapter 8
Afterwards

March-November 1918

Although Jack's great adventure was over, the Great War lasted for another seven and a half months. At first the Germans continued to make speedy progress but this was halted due in part to the stubborn defence by the British and their allies, in part to the exhaustion of the troops, but also the desire of the hungry German troops to eat and drink the plentiful British stores they found, rather than fight. By 5th April, when the Kaiser's Battle which had started on 21st March ended, they had moved forward about 40 miles. Albert had been captured and the major city of Amiens was only 10 miles away but Ludendorff's army was still 50 miles from Paris or the sea; the objectives of the battle had not been achieved. As Martin Middlebrook writes:

> The Allies were left exhausted but not beaten. Their morale was intact and their leadership was united for the first time in the war.[1]

Jack's brigade was pushed back nearly 30 miles by the end of March and for the rest of the war the men were frequently on the move. In mid-April they travelled north to Godwearsvelde, about five miles south of Poperinge, but they seem to have been held in reserve as no fighting is mentioned, although various German assaults were taking place in that area at the same time. The enemy gained about 10 miles of ground but once again the strategic objective of reaching the sea was not achieved.

The 21st Division had not had much luck during the war: it had been mauled at Loos, badly affected by the Battle of the Somme, had taken part in bitter fighting at Arras and Passchendaele and had been directly in the path of the German Spring Offensive.

Then in early May, the division reached what Richard Holmes describes in _Tommy_ as the "very nadir of its bad luck", when it was sent by train over 160 miles south-east to the Champagne region near Reims to rest and was caught up in another German offensive.[2] Here too, the Germans gained some ground but once again their offensive was halted before it became decisive. According to the website of the Western Front Association, this failure was due to similar reasons as their other offensives of 1918:

> _a lack of reserves to follow up the initial penetration, and the excesses of the German frontline troops, as they indulged in an orgy of looting and drunkenness, in a countryside renowned for its rich wine cellars._[3]

In June the 94th Brigade marched 150 miles west to the area near Le Tréport on the coast. After a week it moved a few miles north and by 1st July the brigade was at rest at Vismes au Val when it became immobile due to attack of influenza - early signs of the Spanish Flu epidemic which was to kill millions of people world wide. As a result of the outbreak, on 3rd July the brigade moved to Erondelle, just south of Abbeville:

> _...with the assistance of ambulances and motor lorries. Temporary hospital erected. As many as 200 men all ranks affected with influenza at one time._[4]

They were there for nearly 20 days. During this time, Ludendorff launched what would be his last offensive of the war in the area around Reims. He also planned to re-start the assault in the Somme area, but his attack failed and the Allies were able to counter-attack effectively. For the first time since March the Germans had to retreat.

Once the men of the 94th Brigade were fit again, it moved 30 miles east to Acheux en Amiénois and went into action on 28th July. From then until the end of the war, the brigade took part in the final Allied advance. Progress was slow at first but gathered pace to the extent that in October the Brigade Headquarters changed six times.

In all, by 11th November the brigade had advanced about 63 miles. On route they passed close to Epéhy, before ending up near Berlaimont, south east of Valenciennes.

The diary does not mention the Armistice. Perhaps the men of the brigade were too exhausted to do much celebrating.

On the 4th December H.M. The King inspected the 94th Brigade but by 12th December, the men were on the road again, this time back to La Chaussée southwest of Amiens, not far from where they had started out in July 1918.

For the next four months the brigade stayed in billets. The demobilisation process took some time and the diary describes some of the activities which took place while the men were waiting, for example:

December 1918 - Accommodation for men and horses was poor, necessitating the building of huts for the men while horse lines had to be put on the roads as no other hard ground could be found. Time mostly spent in improving billets and recreation.

February 1919 - Brigade still in billets and huts. Many huts have been erected and the men are much more comfortable now. Recreational training carried out during the whole month, also education facilities are much better.

March 1919 - Brigade sports were held which proved to be fairly successful. Also recreational training was carried out through the whole month.[5]

During this time all the horses used by the army were examined by vets. The best were returned to Britain but the rest were sold locally, often for knock-down prices on a flooded market.[6]

By April 1919 horses and equipment had been sold off and finally the last of the troops were demobilised. Jack's surviving comrades were going home.

Statistics

About a quarter of the adult male population of the UK passed through the army during the Great War, and just over half of these men were volunteers.[7] During the war the 21st Division suffered 55,581 casualties, making it the hardest-hit New Army Division.[8]

From research undertaken, the names of men from Bilsdale who fought in the Great War have been compiled. On the evidence available so far, we know of 41 men who enlisted of whom 14 were killed, but it is impossible to say if this is the total number of enlistments. However, it is still interesting to compare statistics for Bilsdale with those for the country as a whole.

Table 2 - % of 1901 male population who enlisted

	Male population in 1901	Men enlisted from August 1914	% of males who enlisted
England and Wales	15,728,577[9]	4,279,082[10]	27.2
Bilsdale	398[11]	41[12]	10.3

Table 3 - % of enlisted men who were killed

	Men enlisted from August 1914	Men Killed	% killed
British Isles	4,970,902[13]	704,803[14]	14.2
Bilsdale	41[15]	14[16]	34.1

It is interesting to note that fewer men from Bilsdale enlisted compared with the national averages. This can be explained, at least in part, by the fact that agriculture was the most important part of the local economy and that, although not a reserve occupation as in World War Two, agricultural workers could gain an exemption from military service. However, it is much less easy to explain the higher percentage of men from Bilsdale who were killed compared with figures for the whole of the British Isles.

The search for Jack

For a long time after the end of the War, all that was left of Jack were his medals, the 1914-15 Star, the Victory Medal 1914-1918 and the British War Medal 1914-1920, and his "Dead Man's Penny". This plaque was sent to the family of every man who died. There is a family tale that Jack would have been recommended for a gallantry award, but his commanding officer died before the dispatch could be

Jack's Dead Man's Penny

written, but of course there is no way we can prove this.

Jack's Medals

War memorial at St. Hilda's Church

War memorial in Chop Gate village

The only other permanent memorial to Jack was his name engraved on the two war memorials in Chop Gate, one in St. Hilda's Churchyard and one in Chop Gate village. Here Jack's name is written alongside those of eight other men from the Dale who died in the Great War: Harry Ainsley, Percy William Allenby, Charles William Reginald Duncombe, Robert Etherington, Harry Knaggs, William Tasker, Henry Trousdale and Clarence Elwyn Wilson. A further five men, Ernest Allison, Harold Atkinson, John Thomas Garbutt, John William Garbutt and Joseph Garbutt are commemorated at St. John the Divine Church at Fangdale Beck. (See Appendix 2).

Jack's body was, as 2/Lt Frank W Pearse's letter makes clear, never found. We cannot be sure what happened to him but it is most likely that he was killed by the German artillery attack and that his remains were lost as the enemy advanced. This was the case for many men; only 978 of the 7,485 British soldiers killed on 21st March 1918 have an individual identified grave.[17]

Every member of the allied armed forces who was killed in the Great War, is commemorated either on a headstone in one of the thousands of battlefield cemeteries or on a memorial to the missing. These sites are maintained by the Commonwealth War Graves Commission which was established in 1917 to provide a permanent monument to the sacrifice of those who died. Land for this purpose was provided in perpetuity by countries such as France and Belgium, and these spaces are tended by local gardeners with a view to creating the ambiance of an English country garden.

I believe that at some point after the end of the war, Jack's family would have been officially notified about the fact his body had not been found. They would also have been told where he was commemorated, but for whatever reason this information seems to have been lost or forgotten. Perhaps Isaac thought it best not to tell Mary Emma that there was no grave for fear of upsetting her still further and when he died in 1940 the secret died with him.

However, as the years passed it became increasingly important to the family, especially Mary Emma, to find out what had happened to Jack. In July 1950 Jack's sister Gladys visited Holland and Belgium with her younger sister Hannah, and as part of this trip she visited Ypres. She had heard of the Menin Gate and knew that the names of men who had no known grave were commemorated there. In Ypres she spent a long time looking through the 54,896 names on the panels of the memorial but to no avail; as she said:

It was like looking for a needle in a haystack.[18]

When Gladys returned to England she had to make a difficult decision:

We never told my Mother about it or anyone else (in case they conveyed the news to her) as we knew that she would have been broken-hearted had she known that nothing could be found about Jack. It was one of her dearest wishes that someone in the family would visit the area where she imagined Jack's grave could be found but at the time she wouldn't have any idea of the thousands of British Soldiers who were killed during the Somme Battles.[19]

Mary Emma died a few years later in 1959 without knowing where her son was commemorated. I heard this tale in February 1981 when visiting Gladys in Bradford with my family. I had known about Jack from an early age and in 1979, when on a school exchange to Acheux en Amiénois in the Somme, had visited some of the memorials, including the one at Thiépval which has over 73,000 names and where I spent a long time looking for Jack.

What neither Gladys nor I knew was that we were looking in the wrong place; the Menin Gate only lists the names of those men who died in the Ypres area between 1914 and August 1917 and Thiépval only lists those men who died in the Somme battles between July 1916 and 20th March 1918.

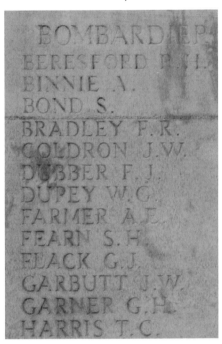

Memorial Plaque at Pozières

When in France I had heard of the Commonwealth War Graves Commission and in March 1981 wrote to them asking for any information about Jack. Ten days later I received a reply which told me exactly where he was commemorated - on a panel in a cemetery in Pozières near Albert which was specially designed as a memorial to those men of the Fifth Army who died between 21st March 1918 and 7th August 1918 who have no known graves. Within weeks of receiving the reply my brother John was due to participate on a similar school exchange to the Somme area. He was able to visit Pozières memorial and take pictures which we sent to Gladys. She wrote:

> It has now given me a lot of peace of mind to know that Jack's name and sacrifice had been remembered ... I am most grateful for these photographs and shall treasure them to the end of my days.[20]

The following year I also had my first chance to visit Pozières when my family visited France on holiday. Gladys asked us to write in the Visitor's Book:

Bombardier John Wm Garbutt, 63978, "C" Battery, 94ᵗʰ Brigade, Royal Field Artillery, Died 21ˢᵗ March 1918 - Treasured memories of a very dear Brother and Uncle. All our Love, Gladys and family.[21]

In 1986, when studying for a university dissertation, I came across the *Official History of the Great War*. From this book I was able to identify where Jack had been on 21ˢᵗ March 1918 and therefore where he had died. This was of great interest to Gladys and was the last information I was able to send her before her death in 1992.

More recently I have transcribed the War Diaries of the 96ᵗʰ, 97ᵗʰ, 94ᵗʰ Brigades and 21ˢᵗ Division which have been used in this book and now know where Jack was and what he and his comrades were doing on any given date of the war. Sadly, I discovered these documents after the deaths of all of Jack's siblings, but I know that Gladys would have been delighted to read it and know more about her brother's service.

Since I became a teacher, Jack has been a regular feature of school assemblies. I have also spoken to students about him when on language learning visits to France, which often included visits to the battlefields. More recently, on visits with the main objective of teaching students about the history of the Great War, I have had the privilege of telling students about Jack's life and death while standing in front of his memorial in Pozières.

Finally, in 2003 I visited the area around Epéhy where Jack died. It was a cold February day and the area is very exposed with few trees to give shelter from the icy wind. I imagine very little has changed in this respect since 1918.

During this visit I went to Ste. Emilie Valley Cemetery. This was the site of the grave of the only other person from the 94ᵗʰ Brigade who died on 21ˢᵗ March 1918, Lance Bombardier

R. Oakley of "D" Battery. The Commonwealth War Graves Commission website describes the burials in this cemetery:

> *On the site of this cemetery at the Armistice, there were three large graves of Commonwealth soldiers buried by the Germans, which now form part of Plot I. The remainder of the cemetery is composed almost entirely of graves brought in from an older cemetery of the same name or from the Battlefields.*[22]

I thought that perhaps Jack's body lay in an unmarked grave near that of L/Bdr Oakley, both bodies being brought in from the battlefields after the war, but Jack's not being identified.

I found the Oakley headstone easily and only a few graves away, came across the stone pictured on page 215.

Of course, like so many things in this story, it is impossible to be certain but there are 22 Bombardiers of the Royal Field Artillery commemorated at Pozières who have no known grave and a further 17 on the Vis-en-Artois memorial which commemorates those who fell during the final Allied advance. If one discounts those men who were fighting at some distance (more than about 8 miles) from Ste. Emilie, then there is perhaps a one in eleven chance that this is Jack's grave. Perhaps, at last, his final resting place has been found.

Jack's Legacy

My Great-Uncle Jack died 90 years ago and as far as I know there is no-one still alive who actually knew him. His mother died without knowing what had happened to him and making sure his sister was able to see a photograph of his name on a memorial before her death is very important to me.

I hope that in some small way the research I have done into his life and death means that Jack's name will live on. It is important that people know what he and millions of other men like him went through during the First World War in the name of freedom - from the disaster of Loos, to the carnage of the Somme, to the mud of Passchendaele, ending in the near defeat of the Spring Offensive. When men have given their lives in such a way it is vital that:

> *At the going down of the sun and in the morning*
> *We will remember them.*[23]

Headstone with the inscription,
"A Bombardier of the Great War", Ste. Emilie Valley Cemetery

94th Brigade RFA, War Diary
April 1918 – April 1919
April 1918; Lt Col HA Boyd; BEAUCOURT; Sheet 62D

1   Brigade less B Battery at rest at BEAUCOURT. B Battery who were in action south east of BRESLE under 95th Brigade were withdrawn over night and rested in wagon lines at BAIZIEUX.

2   All Batteries into billets at FRECHENCOURT. HQ remained at BEAUCOURT SUR HALLUE.

4   Brigade under command of 4th Australian Division. Moved at 4.30pm into position of observation north west of CORBIE. Battery positions were at I26 and 32 covering front between VAIRE SOUS CORBIE and the BOIS de VAIRE. HQ at ESCARDONNEUSE. Wagon lines at QUERRIEU (I15 central).

6   Brigade under command of 33rd Australian Division.

9   Brigade withdrew to wagon lines.

11   9am - Brigade marched to GUIZANCOURT near DOULLENS where it went into billets. *21st DA OO*.

13-14 Brigade entrained at DOULLENS and detrained at GODWEARSVELDE. Positions taken north of FLETRE in W4, 5 and 6. Under tactical command of 133rd French Division and superimposed over the front south west of METEREN. Wagon lines at P7, 19 and 24, Sheet 28. HQ at Q33b.5.5.

19   Brigade moved with 133rd French Division to a sector further north and Batteries went into action north of MONT ROUGE and were superimposed on front north of BAILLEUL, sheet 27. Wagon lines near WEST OUTRE, sheet 28. HQ at R18c.6.4.

23-24 Moved overnight to positions south west of BERTHEN and covered the same front as before. Wagon lines near GODWEARSVELDE. HQ at R20c, sheet 27.

Cas   1 2/Lt R TOWNROW (A) wounded (gas).

16 Sgt R McINNES (C) wounded but at duty.

17 Dr JW GRICE (B) wounded.

20 Dr R ADAMS (B) wounded.

21 Gnr JP WICKS (B), Gnr EG MATHEWS (B), Gnr W ARNOLD (B) all killed.

23 S/S D SMITH (D), Bdr HW WELSH (D) both wounded but at duty.

25 Sgt WE HASLEDEN (B) wounded (shell shock), L/Bdr H HENSBY (B) wounded, Gnr EC REEKS (B) wounded, Gnr AE WINGATE (B), Gnr T KETTERICK (B), Major GEW FRANKLYN (B) all wounded but all duty.

26 2/Lt WW COMPTON (C) killed, Gnr EC MARKHAM (C) wounded. L/Bdr W RILEY (C), Gnr A BOYCE (C), Gnr WH DRAKE (C), Gnr HW SMITH (C) all wounded (gas).

29 Gnr O JONES (A) killed, Gnr L JOHNSTON (A) wounded, L/Bdr H HENSBY (B) died of wounds.

Hons   Cpl EA SAMPSON (HQ) Bar to Military Medal, Gnr D LESLIE (A) Military Medal, Dr FG GRIGGS (A) Military Medal, Sgt T CURTIS (C) Military Medal, Cpl H GILBERT (C) Military Medal, Dr G HAVRON (C) Military Medal, Dr WJ DEAN (C) Military Medal, Dr R JONES (C) Military Medal, Bdr JW FOSTER (D) Military Medal, Cpl EE ALLEN (D) Military Medal, Bdr JH HAYDON (D) Military Medal, Gnr NW PERROTT (D) Military Medal.

May 1918; Lt Col HA Boyd; BERTHEN district

1   Batteries in action south west of BERTHEN covering front held by 133rd French Division. HQ on southern slope of MONT DES CATS. Wagon lines in GODWEARSVELDE district.

4   Support given in early morning to a local enterprise with 133rd French Division which proved successful.

	Noon - Batteries pulled out and marched to ST MOMELIN near ST OMER. Encamped for night.
5	Brigade entrained at ARQUES and WIZERNES.
6-7	Sgt W JAMESON (B) and Sgt WE HASLEDEN (B) awarded Military Medal. Detrained at SERZY ET PRIN and marched to rest camps at LHERY (SOISSONS map).
8	Gnr G MARPLES awarded Military Medal.
13	11am - Brigade marched to ETRIGNY and went into halting stage camps.
15	Brigade relieved 74th French Divisional Artillery in sector north of LONRE. Batteries took up positions in the vicinity of HERMONVVILLE and CAYROY. HQ at ST AUBOEUF, wagon lines remaining at TRIGNY.
16	Sgt LJ CARDY (D) DCM, 2/Lt GP CHAPMAN (A) DSO, Maj CW ALLFREY (C) Bar to Military Medal, Cap JM McNEILL (A) Military Cross, Lt O MURRAY-LYON (D) Military Cross, 2/Lt W CRAMPTON (A) Military Cross, 2/Lt J CALDER (B) Military Cross. Gnr A ROBINSON (A) Military Medal, L/Bdr W AUDSLEY (A) Military Medal, Gnr WA PAMLEY (A) Military Medal.
18	Wagon lines moved to camps about 1 mile south of BOUVANCOURT on the BOUVANCOURT-JONCHERY road.
26	As a result of news from prisoners that the enemy was planning an attack, all Batteries carried out counter preparation fire from 10pm.
27	1am - very heavy HE and gas shell bombardment. From then until 8am Batteries continued to fire on Z barrage lines. 8am - fire was changed to Y barrage. Enemy progress forced Batteries to withdraw to positions on ridge near ST AUBOEUF from 11.30am. Last Battery withdrawn about 3pm. All Batteries in action at new position by 6pm. Further withdrawal at 8.30pm to positions near TRIGNY.

28   10am - enemy reported to be near crest west of TRIGNY. *21 DA order C2,* SOISSONS map. A and C Batteries withdrawn to CHALONS SUR VESLE. B and D withdrawn later to positions west of CHALONS SUR VESLE.
12.30pm - orders received that next position would be west of ROSNAY. B Battery sent at once. Others followed at 1 hour intervals.

29   Excellent positions found and effective work done due to good observation until midday when further withdrawal commenced as enemy gaining ground rapidly in direction of TRESLON. Intermediate position taken up half mile north west of MERY PREMECY and later, at about 6pm, all Batteries withdrawn to VILLERS FARM half mile south west of ST EUPHRAISE to cover TRESLON RIDGE.

30   9am - Batteries moved to position north east of BLIGNY and covered 19th Division owing to enemy advance from SARCY.
11pm - Batteries withdrew and came into action by order of 21st DA near POURCY.

31   Orders received for all 18pdr Batteries to take up positions between COURMASSU and the BOIS du PETIT CHAMP and cover line between AUBILLY and BLIGNY held by 28th French Division. Position occupied by noon. D Battery remained in POURCY as no 4.5 How ammunition was available. Wagon lines half way between FLEURY and NANTEUIL.

Cas   5 Gnr N MORRIS (C) wounded (gas).
27 L/Bdr A KAY (A), Gnr T WEAVERS (A), Gnr J CHRISTAIN (A), Gnr R FITZSIMMONS (A), Gnr J RAYNOR (A) all wounded (gas). Maj CW ALFREY (A) wounded (gas) but remained at duty. Sgt WG PATTENDEN (C) wounded in action. Cpl TJ SMITH (C), Gnr FE BOWELL (C), Gnr JT CROSS (C), Gnr C WIGGENS (C), Gnr E FOX (C), Dr TA LENHAM (C), all wounded. L/Bdr WG GILES (C), Gnr H

WEAVER (C), Dr JGR COOK (C) all wounded (gas) but remained at duty. Bdr JA PALMER (C) died of wounds. Gnr H TURNER (C), Dr J HARVEY (C), S/S WJ RIDGE (D) all killed in action. Sgt WJ SMITH (AVC) (D), Gnr R WATT (D), Dr W PAYNE (D), Cpl WG JONES (D) all wounded.

June 1918; Major H Corry; SOISSONS; sheet 22

3	D Battery came into action in BOIS de REIMS alongside all other Batteries. All wagon lines moved to ST IMOGES.
5	All Batteries moved back to supporting position in BOIS de POURCY.
14	Brigade relieved at 11pm by 3rd group of 228th French and withdrew to wagon lines.
15	Brigade moved to GOINGES.
16	Brigade moved to CONNANTRAY.
17	Brigade moved to MAILLY LE CAMP.
18	Entrained at SOUSES-SOUS.
19	Detrained at LONGPRE.
20	Moved to ERONDELLE area.
21	Moved to BOULLANCOURT area.
22	Moved to EU.
30	Moved to MARTAINVILLE area.
Cas	1 Gnr J McDOOUGALL (A), Gnr FA SALVIDGE (B) wounded.
	3 Sgt GS BAKER (D) and Gnr C DICKMAN (D) wounded.
	5 Sgt J LYDON (A), Gnr S SWAN (B) wounded.
	6 Sgt W JAMESON (C) wounded.
	9 Dr Q FOY (B), Gnr W LEE (B), Bdr J GILMAN (B), Bdr W BUCK (B), Gnr EE ELKINS (D), Gnr A REED (D), all wounded. Gnr A BADLAND (D) wounded but at duty.
	10 2/Lt GP CHAPMAN (A), Gnr W PAMLEY (A) wounded.

Hons   Lt PME BROWNLOW (B) Military Cross, Lt JA STITT (B) Military Cross, Gnr JW ATKINSON Military Medal, Dr W THOMPSON Military Medal, Dr R WILLETS Military Medal, Dr J ARTHURS Military Medal, Dr JA BREARLY Military Medal, Dr J WATSON Military Medal, Bdr W ATKINSON Military Medal, Sgt J WHITE Military Medal, Gnr C ROSS Military Medal, Bdr EH TAYLOR Military Medal.

July 1918; Lt/Col HA Boyd; ABBEVILLE

1   Brigade at rest at VISMES AU VAL where it became immobile due to attack of influenza.

3   Moved to ERONDELLE with the assistance of ambulances and motor lorries. Temporary hospital erected. As many as 200 men from all ranks affected with influenza at one time.

22   Leaving ERONDELLE at 9.30am, Brigade marched to CANAPLES and billeted. *21st DA order no 30.*

23   Starting at 9am, Brigade marched to near RAINCHEVAL. Horse lines situated at N11b and N12a. Billets obtained in RAINCHEVAL (sheet 57D).

27   Evening - *21st DA order 32*, the Brigade commenced relief of 121st Brigade RFA. Wagon lines moved to ACHEUX, covering the HAMEL front of V corps HQ at P24d.4.4.

28   Take over from 121st Brigade completed at 7pm. Much harassing fire carried out each night.

30   Bombardment of enemy line first with smoke shell commencing 9am. Followed at 9.10am for 15 minutes and 9.55am for 5 minutes by shrapnel and HE. *21st DA no 33.*

Cas   0

August 1918; Lt Col HA Boyd; HQ at P24d.3.5, sheet 57D

1-20   Brigade covered right half of 21st Division front opposite HAMEL (ANCRE). Batteries disposed in depth near ENGLEBELMER at ranges varying from 3300 to 5000 yards from enemy lines. All Batteries had a detached section in forward position and this used for harassing fire day and night. Early part of month, targets were crossings of River ANCRE opposite divisional front and roads leading thereto. Later, after enemy had evacuated HAMEL, fire directed on trenches, roads and tracks around THIEPVAL, THIEPVAL WOOD and ST PIERRE DIVION.

20   Batteries moved forward to positions in valley running northwards from MESNIL Q22 and 28 for offensive operation. One section of B/94 left in old forward positions for harassing fire.

21-24   Infantry attacks started on 21st were only partly successful until 24th when 64th Infantry Brigade succeeded in establishing themselves on high ground south of MIRAUMONT after forcing a crossing of ANCRE at GRANDCOURT. All Batteries now out of range therefore moved to eastern slopes of ARTILLERY VALLEY in R2a and e. Batteries moved at 2 hour intervals starting with B Battery at 10.30am, then C, D and A, due to congestion of roads around BEAUMONT HAMEL and BEAUCOURT. HQ at P24d.3.5.

        4.30pm - B and C Battery ready to fire. D and A arrived but Infantry had advanced further to within a few hundred yards of BAPAUME-ALBERT road west of LE SARS. New position therefore out of range. Decided to come into action on crest of high ground south of MIRAUMONT by dawn to support attack on LE SARS. Night spent in bivouacs in ARTILLERY VALLEY.

25   7am - all Batteries in action from positions on or near west MIRAUMONT road about R11 central. Good observation. Many fleeting targets in and about DESTREMONT farm and LE SARS were successfully engaged during day. These captured towards evening. Preparations made for further advance next day. HQ at R10b.2.8.

26   Positions taken astride AQUEDUCT road west of LE SARS to support attacks aiming to capture BEAULENCOURT and crossing of BAPAUME-PERONNE road. Rather more opposition than expected in sunken road near LUISENHOF FARM and line on high ground west of BEAULENCOURT not established until following day. HQ at M8d.8.6.

28   Brigade took up positions of readiness near EAUCOURT L'ABBAYE. Placed under orders of GOC 64th Infantry Brigade in support to 110th Infantry Brigade. No firing from these positions. HQ at M17b.4.1.

31   HQ at N13d. To assist in attack on BEAULENCOURT in evening and on sugar factory on the following morning, Batteries moved to positions 1000 - 1500 yards north of GUEUDECOURT-LIGNY-TAILLOY road. Evening attack did not succeed.

Cas   2 Gnr C ROSS (C) wounded (gas).
5 Gnr F MADDOCK (C) wounded (gas).
6 Gnr W JORDAN (C) wounded (gas).
7 Gnr B WARD (C) killed.
14 Gnr WHITTAKER (C), Bdr G CARTER (C), Gnr H BURROWS (C) all wounded (gas).
26 Sgt EE ALLEN (D), Bdr A FELDON (D), Bdr J MOSLEY (D), Gnr J WOOD (D) all wounded. Dr A HADDON (B) wounded.
27 Gnr C KING (B) wounded but remained at duty.

September 1918; Lt/Col HA Boyd; LUISENHOF FARM; Sheet 57C

1/2   Batteries from positions north of GUEUDECOURT supported a successful attack by the 64th Brigade on the CLAY PIT, 013a.4.2, and LUBDA COPSE.

2/3   An attack by 110th Infantry Brigade on BEAULENCOURT succeeded in taking the village. Batteries were moved to positions west of BEAULENCOURT, N18d and 24b, early on the morning of the 3rd. *21st DA order.*

3   HQ at Sunken Road N24a. Brigade came under the tactical control of the CRA 17th Division. Owing to the rapid retirement of the enemy, Batteries were out of range by midday. Brigade remained in these positions of observation.

4   HQ at Gun Pits O28b.1.8. Orders from CRA 17th Division were received about 9am for the Brigade to come into positions of readiness about O22 and 28. At 2.30pm, owing to the Infantry situation being obscure, orders were received from 17th Divisional Artillery to come into action in positions of observation in the neighbourhood of the positions of readiness. Positions were taken up in O22d and O28a. From here attacks by the 17th Division Infantry on trench system between YTRES and ETRICOURT were supported.

5   During the night the position of A Battery was changed as ammunition supply to position at first occupied was impossible under cover. At the request of the Infantry, heavy fire was directed on specified trenches frequently during the day. At 5.30pm and 8.30pm barrages were fired to support our attack. HQ at site of Chateau SAILLY SAILLISEL. In accordance with the 17th DA instructions, Battery positions were exchanged with the 121st Brigade RFA. The exchange took place between 8pm

and midnight. Owing to the intense darkness and heavy rains, Batteries in some cases did not get into their new positions until day break on 6th inst. New positions taken up were east of SAILLY SAILLISEL in U15, 16 and 18.

6   HQ at Gun Pits X14a. The enemy having retired from the canal at MANANCOURT, the Brigade was ordered forward to east of the canal and Batteries took up positions in V14b and d and 20a. The Brigade again came under orders of 21st DA and supported the 62nd Infantry Brigade. During the night of 6/7 EQUANCOURT, FINS and SOREL were occupied by our infantry.

7   HQ at V17d.8.5. Batteries were moved forward to positions south of SOREL LE GRAND in V24b and d covering HEUDECOURT. From these positions attacks were supported which resulted in the capture of REVELON FARM.

9   A, C and D Batteries were moved forward to positions south of HEUDECOURT to support an attack on CHAPEL HILL. The attack failed.

16   B Battery which had remained behind the other Batteries of the Brigade in position south of SOREL LE GRAND moved forward to W27a with a view to an operation to take CHAPEL HILL and the ridge between there and PEIZIERES.

17   To be in close liaison with 62nd Infantry Brigade for operations the following day, Brigade HQ moved about 9pm to the BRICK YARD south of HEUDECOURT (W21d).

18   For this attack the 315th and 72nd Army Brigades RFA came under command of OC 94th Brigade RFA. The first phase of the attack in the early morning was entirely successful. Batteries were moved forward one by one at intervals during the day to positions south of CHAPEL HILL in W24a and c with a view to supporting further advance of our Infantry.

19   The 110th and 64th Infantry Brigades having taken over the Divisional front from 62nd Infantry Brigade, HQ for purpose of close liaison were moved forward to dugouts partly occupied by the 110th Infantry Brigade at W18d.1.2. During the night 19th/20th the 19th Infantry Brigade (33rd Division) took over the line from 110th Infantry Brigade.

20   The 94th Brigade RFA came under tactical control of CRA 33rd Division at 10am. Close liaison was maintained with 19th Infantry Brigade and later 100th Infantry Brigade until arrival of Artillery Brigades of 33rd Division on 23rd. During this period artillery support was given to several enterprises attempted at different times by 33rd Divisional Infantry, having as their objective the capture of VILLERS GUISLAIN, MEATH POST, MEATH LANE and LIMERICK POST. None of these attacks were successful.

23   In accordance with 33rd DA orders, Brigade HQ at W18d.1.2 were handed over to 156th Brigade RFA and the late HQ of 315th Army Brigade RFA at W22d were occupied. The duties of liaison with 100th Infantry Brigade passed to OC 156th Brigade at 7.30pm on 23rd.

26   A single gun for sniping and anti-tank work was placed in position about X25b central.

28   A general attack carried out in the early morning in conjunction with Divisions on right and left succeeded in clearing the enemy from VILLERS GUISLAIN and all the high ground west of CANAL de ST QUENTIN. Elements of the enemy were believed to be still in trenches just west of the canal. A and D Batteries were moved about midday to positions east of PEZIERE in X19d. B Battery followed during the night of 28th/29th and came into action at X25b.

29   During the early hours of the morning the fact was established that the enemy had evacuated all ground west of the canal between HONNECOURT and

VENDHUILE. Our 18 pdr Batteries placed single guns in forward positions just west of canal about X17a.

30   Attempts made by 100th Infantry Brigade to push patrols across the canal in direction of LATERRIERE were frustrated by the enemy machine gunners on the east bank of canal. Sniping was carried out by Batteries from forward guns during the day with good results.

Cas   4 Cap L ADAMS (A) and Dr A SMITH (A) both wounded in action.

16 Sgt LJ CARDY (D) wounded in action.

19 Sgt VERNUM (B), Cpl DOAD (B), Bdr BROWN (B), Gnr SMITH (B), Gnr SIDES (B), Gnr GILLESPIE (B), Gnr J TIERNEY (D) all wounded in action.

24 Maj CW ALLFREY (C), Capt RAHS GEADES (C), Lt R HERON (C), 2/Lt JJ MELLON (C), 2/Lt GM COATS (C), Dr SE WILLIS? (C), Dr WA HOLDWAY (C), Bdr WH DRAKE (C), Gnr C LONG (C), Gnr L KITCHEN (C), Gnr F TALYOR (C), Gnr S THORPE (C), Gnr AP SAMME (C), Dr A STEWART (C), Maj CM TAYLOR (D) all wounded in action (gas).

Hons   Gnr F BUDGEN (A) Military Medal, Dr A WOOLLANS (A) Military Medal, Gnr C ROSS (C) Croix de Guerre, L/Bdr F TAYLOR (D) Croix de Guerre, Dr C HADDON (B) Military Medal.

October 1918; Major HC Colliver; PEZIERE VILLERS-GUISLAN Road

1-5   Brigade under 33rd Division was in position in vicinity of QUAIL Valley east of PEZIERE. Enemy retired from HINDENBURG system on the front covered by the Brigade during the 4th/5th October. Orders were received during the evening for the Brigade to move across the CANAL de ST QUENTIN at BANTEUX in support of the 110th Infantry Brigade which was in reserve.

6   HQ at M22b.7.1. Brigade again came under the command of CRA 21st Division. Batteries moved independently at dawn to a rendezvous at BANTOUZELLE. As a result of reconnaissance during the morning, positions were selected south of VAUCELLES WOOD and occupied during the afternoon. The order at that point was for only two Batteries (B & D) to take up their positions but this was countermanded with the result that A & D came into action just before dark. D Battery was detailed to cut wire of the WALINCOURT-AUDIGNY line on the southern part of divisional front.

7   HQ at S4a.8.5. D Battery continued wire cutting.

8   Barrages were fired 01.00, 05.15 and 08.00 hours. One section from A Battery and two sections from C Battery were sent forward to support battalions of 62nd Infantry Brigade who carried out the attack which commenced at 08.00 hours. Close liaison was maintained with Battalion commanders all day and much useful work was done. This was more especially so in the case of the section from A Battery under the command of 2/Lt CHAPMAN DSO which on one occasion turned captured 77mm guns on the enemy with great effect. At about 09.30 hours Batteries were moved forward to positions in N26. A barrage was commenced at 18.00 hours in support of an attack on WALINCOURT but this was stopped at 18.25 hours as it was found that our infantry had already occupied the village.

9   HQ at MONTECOUVEY FARM. Orders were received overnight to the effect that the 21st Divisional Artillery would come under the control of CRA 17th Division at 05.00 hours. The Brigade was placed at the disposal of the 17th Divisional Artillery for an early morning attack on the high ground N18a, north of SELVIGNY. This attack was cancelled as it was found that the enemy had gone

further back during the night. The Brigade was ordered at 08.00 hours to reconnoitre positions in N17, 23 or 29 and to occupy these as soon as GARE WOOD was held by our troops. Orders received from 17th Divisional Artillery at 09.00 hours to move Batteries to position in abovementioned squares at once as CAULLERY was now in our hands. When reconnoitring parties arrived on the high ground in N18a at about 10.30 hours it was seen that the enemy had gone much further back and the Batteries would consequently be out of effective range if they came into action in the position which had been ordered. Batteries were therefore ordered to rendezvous north of SELVIGNY and a reconnoitring party under the Brigade commander went forward to high ground between CAULLERY and MONTIGNY. As a result of this reconnaissance A Battery was brought into action east of CAULLERY (O9a.8.2) and the remaining Batteries moved to position of readiness on the NW edge of the village of CAULLERY. From their positions A Battery did some excellent sniping during the afternoon on the area between CAUDRY and LETRONQUOY FARM.

10 Brigade formed part of main body and was instructed not to move without orders from 17th Divisional Artillery. At 01.00 hours the Brigade was ordered to position of readiness near MONTIGNY. On arrival of reconnoitring parties there, further orders were issued by 17th DA for Batteries to come into action on T22c on the southern outskirts of INCHY to fire a barrage at 17.00 hours around NEUVILLY where resistance had been met. Roads were very much congested and it was only by going across country through a great deal of ploughed fields that Batteries were able to get into positions in time. No registrations were carried out but the 50th Infantry Brigade expressed their satisfaction at the barrage.

The attack was not successful. New troops of a Jaeger regiment were met who put up a very strong resistance with the result that after the village on both flanks, our troops were forced to retire to the line of the river. NEUVILLY was reported to be a veritable nest of MG. Batteries were shelled intermittently during the night by 8" Howitzers. A Battery, who were forced to withdraw temporarily from their position, had one gun put out of action and some ammunition blown up. Horses and mules were now very exhausted as a result of continuous heavy work during the past seven weeks.

11   HQ at INCHY. No further attempt was made during the day by the infantry to take NEUVILLY. Batteries registered and did a little sniping during the morning and early afternoon. Visibility became very poor at 15.00 hours.

12   Orders received at 02.15 hours for an attack to be carried out by 52nd Infantry Brigade in conjunction with 33rd Division with the object of taking NEUVILLY and high ground east of it. Barrage opened at 05.00 hours and continued until 06.12 hours. The area K10a and K4c was kept under to assist a further operation by 52nd Brigade.

13-15   Only sniping and harassing fire. Visibility generally very poor. During the night 15th/16th October the village of INCHY and the surroundings, including Battery positions, was heavily shelled with mustard gas. Considering the intensity of the bombardment the number of casualties in the Brigade was very small. Heavy rain from about dawn and a liberal use of Chloride of Lime undoubtedly prevented the developments.

16   Gas shell at last became available for the 18pdrs. 1100 rounds of "BB" were drawn by the Brigade.

17   Shoots were carried out by Batteries as follows: 00.05 - 00.30 hours - Gas shoot on SUNKEN ROAD and TRAMWAY in K3d and K9b. Burst of harassing fire of 5 minutes

duration at 03.45 and 04.30 hours. In conjunction with an operation carried out by 4th Army, a Chinese barrage was put down east of NEUVILLY from 07.42 - 08.24 hours. The morning turned very foggy at about 07.00 hours and it was only with great difficulty that Batteries were able to lay their guns.

18 Batteries moved at intervals between dawn and 09.00 hours to positions in J18c and J24b behind the crest, about 3000 yards west of NEUVILLY.

19 The day was spent in getting up large quantities of ammunition and in generally preparing for the attack timed for the following morning. Concentrations of 5 minutes were fired at 06.00, 10.25, and 22.50 hours on points of probable resistance.

20 Barrage opened at 02.00 hours and continued until 08.05 hours. The object of the attack, which was carried out in four stages, was to take AMERVAL and the high ground east of NEUVILLY. About 09.00 hours fire was concentrated on the left of the divisional front against a counter attack which was developing. This counter attack was stopped. Owing to bad visibility and the constant fluctuation of the line due to small local counter attacks, the situation was not clear until late in the evening when it was found that the final objective had been taken throughout except for a pocket in AMERVAL. Orders were received about 16.30 hours for the Brigade to cross the River SERRE overnight and to come into action at dawn on the rising ground north east of NEUVILLY.

21 Batteries moved at about 04.00 hours in a downpour of rain. The bridge north of NEUVILLY by which the Brigade was ordered to cross the river SERRE led on to a ploughed field. Here guns and wagons, even with 12 and 16 horse teams, got stuck fast in the soft ground. In most cases

wagons had to be unloaded and the ammunition sent to the gun positions by pack animals. Brigade again came under orders of the CRA 21st Division at 12.00 hours.

23 HQ at NEUVILLY. The Brigade did not take part in the barrage which opened at 02.00 hours but stood ready to go forward to positions from which it could support 62nd Brigade in the 3rd and 4th phases of the attack, the objects of which were the capture of VENDEGIES and POIX DU NORD. Batteries rendezvoused in positions of readiness between AMERVAL and OVILLERS at 07.00 hours. B & C Batteries moved forward into action south of OVILLERS at about 11.00 hours and were followed by A & D Batteries just before dusk. For all operations after the initial phase of the attack on this day, 95th, 78th, 79th Brigades RFA, the 34th Army FA Brigade, 2 sections of the 135th Brigade RGA (60pdrs) and 6 mobile TMs were placed under the control of the OC 94th Brigade, RFA (Lt Col BOYD DSO). Sections of A & C Batteries were detailed to keep in close support of 1st and 2nd Lincs battalions respectively. Close touch was maintained by these sections with battalion commanders all day but opportunities for effective (Fire?? action??) were few owing to poor visibility and nature of ground. HQ were established at OVILLERS during the evening.

24 HQ at OVILLERS. An attack at 04.00 hours on POIX DU NORD by 62nd and 64th Infantry Brigades was supported by fire from all Batteries. This attack succeeded and A, B and D Batteries moved forward to positions east of VENDEGIES just in time to fire a barrage for an attack at 16.00 hours to capture ground of tactical importance east of POIX DU NORD. C Battery, which had become much reduced in personnel owing to evacuations due to influenza, did not move forward from its positions in OVILLERS.

26/27 Barrage fired at 01.00 hours in support of attack by 110th Infantry Brigade to establish posts on a line approximately from S13d.4.3 to X11b.3.0. At 13.00 hours orders were received for the Brigade to withdraw to CLARY for three days rest. Batteries moved independently during the afternoon and arrived at CLARY between 22.00 and 01.00 hours. Fairly good billets were obtained; officers and NCOs in houses, OR in straw barns.

30 The Brigade returned to the line arriving between 20.00 hours. A, B and D Batteries retuned to the position NE of VENDEGIES which they had vacated on 26th inst. C Battery took up a position in the same vicinity.

31 Harassing fire was carried out by all Batteries at the rate of 300 rounds per 18pdr and 200 rounds per Howitzer Battery per day.

Cas 1 Gnr GA THOMAS (D) wounded.

4 Cpl E CROWNSHAW (C), Gnr R TURNER (C), Bdr RW BARKER (C) killed. Gnr S SCHOFIELD (C), Gnr AE WOODBURN (C), Gnr HH BROWN (C), wounded. Gnr S THORPE (C) "died" (gas).

8 Cpl T MOORE (D), Gnr D WALKER (D) wounded.

10 Gnr C EVANS (D) wounded.

16 Gnr P SMEE (B), Cpl BECKLEY (B), Bdr GRAMHAM (B) wounded (gas).

17 Gnr R KELLY (B), Gnr BROWNING (B) wounded (gas). Gnr G BLAYLOCK (D) wounded (gas?).

19 Bdr H AUDSLEY (A), Sgt E BALSOM (B) wounded (gas).

21 Dr E NICHOLS (B) wounded (gas).

22 Dr G RICE (A), killed. Bdr W TALBOT (D), Gnr J SAVAGE (D), Gnr GH TODD (D) wounded (gas).

23 Dr S EDWARDS (A) wounded.

24 Cpl C OVERTON (B), Gnr READYOUGH (B), Gnr WJ WATTS (B), Gnr RS COOPER (B) wounded. Sgt CURLEY (D) wounded (gas?).

25 Gnr D GRAY (D) wounded (gas?).
30 Sgt G UNDERWOOD (A) killed. Sgt E IBERTSON (A), Gnr NS CANN (A), Gnr W HART (A), Gnr AE LEE (A), Dr T PICKERING (A), Gnr W TRIGGLE (A) wounded.

November 1918; Major HC Colliver; VENDEGIES

1   Brigade was in action near VENDEGIES-AU-BOIS.
3   Brigade moved to forward positions SE of POIX DU NORD during the afternoon and came under the tactical control of CRA 17th Division.
4   HQ at POIX DU NORD. Barrage fired from 15.30 - 23.00 hours in support of attack on FORET DE MORMAL.
4-7   Owing to a very severe epidemic of influenza which had broken out in all Batteries rendering them immobile, orders were received for the Brigade to remain at POIX DU NORD. Batteries moved into the village and wagon lines joined the Batteries on the 5th.
8   HQ at LA GRAND CARRIERE. Orders were received overnight that owing to the difficulty of supplies the Brigade would move forward to LOCQUIGNOL, or further if the situation permitted. Batteries marched at 10.00 hours in to the neighbourhood of BERLAIMONT. Accommodation for one Battery only was available at BERLAIMONT and the Brigade, less A Battery, moved to billets at LA GRAND CARRIERE.
9-14   HQ B, C and D Batteries remained at LA GRAND CARRIERE, A Battery at BERLAIMONT.
15   Orders had been received the previous day for the Brigade to move to billets at NEUVILLY. Owing to the congestion of traffic on the roads the march was carried out by night, commencing at 23.15 hours.

16   HQ at NEUVILLY. The Brigade arrived at NEUVILLY at 05.00 hours and occupied billets.

17-30   Batteries carried out schemes of training. A and D Batteries were inspected by the CRA on 25th November, and B and C Batteries on 26th November.

28   Lt Col HA BOYD DSO awarded the Chevalier du Legion d'Honneur.

Cas   3 Bdr JW EYRES (B) wounded in action. Dr R WILLETS (B) wounded in action (gas).

December 1918; Lt Col HA Boyd; NEUVILLY

1-12   Brigade in billets. Batteries continued with schemes of training. On 4th HM The King visited NEUVILLY and inspected the Brigade.

13   Brigade moved to WALINCOURT at 08.00 hours via TROISVILLES, CLARY and SELVIGNY. Brigade reached WALINCOURT at about 14.30 hours and occupied billets.

14   Brigade moved to BRUSLE at 07.30 hours via VILLERS-OUTREAUX, VEDHUILE, ROISEL and TINCOURT. Brigade reached BRUSLE at 16.00 hours and occupied huts and bivouacs.

15   Brigade moved to PROYART at 08.00 hours via BRIE and FOUCANCOURT. Reached PROYART about 15.00 hours and occupied billets and bivouacs.

16   Brigade moved to BLAGNY at 07.30 hours via VILLERS-BRETTONNEUX. Reached BLAGNY at 14.00 hours and occupied huts.

17   Brigade moved to LA CHAUSSEE at 07.30 hours avoiding AMIENS by the south. Reached LA CHAUSSEE at 13.00 hours.

18-31   Brigade in billets at LA CHAUSSEE. Accommodation for men and horses was poor, necessitating the building of huts for the men while horse lines had to be put on the roads as no other hard ground could be found. Time mostly spent in improving billets and recreation.

Hons Lt Col HA BOYD DSO (HQ) awarded CMG. 2/Lt GP CHAPMAN DSO (A) awarded Military Cross.

Cas 0

January 1919; Lt Col HA Boyd; LA CHAUSSEE; Sheet 62E 1/40000

1-31 Brigade still in billets and huts. Many huts have been erected and the men are much more comfortable now. Recreational training carried out during the whole month, also education facilities are much better.

16 Brigade sent 120 horses to AMIENS for sale.

Cas 0

February 1919; Major FW Hume; LA CHAUSSEE; Sheet 62E 1/40000

1-31
(sic) Brigade still in billets and huts. Nothing of special interest has occurred during the month. Animals were sold at AMIENS, POIX and HORNOY.

15 Brigade reduced to Cadre "B" at about this date.

25 Brigade sports were held which proved to be fairly successful. Also recreational training was carried out through the whole month.

Cas 0

March 1919; 2/Lt D M Webster; LA CHAUSSEE; Sheet 62E 1/40000

1-31   Brigade still in billets and huts. Nothing of special interest has occurred during the month. All guns and vehicles were taken down to Cadre Park LONGPRE with the exception of water-carts. Mobilization stores were also taken to Cadre Park and arranged for inspection by Ordnance. Lt RS KING took up the duties of Sub-Area Commandant LONGPRE, also an officer was detailed to be in charge of the Brigade stores at the Cadre Park LONGPRE. Recreational training is still being carried out but on a rather small scale.

22   The Brigade was reduced to Cadre A at about this date. All remaining horses were sold at sales administered by ADVS V Corps.

Cas   0

April 1919; Major HC Colliver; LA CHAUSSEE

1-4   Brigade fully reduced to Cadre A. All vehicles with the exception of water-carts were removed to Cadre Park LONGPRE, along with all mobilization stores.

4-30   Brigade moved to LONGPRE on the morning of 4th and occupied billets the same night. Recreational training carried out on a very small scale, but the men appear to be fairly comfortable. Nothing more of special interest has occurred during the month.

25   Inspection of mobilization stores at the Cadre Park was carried out by Ordnance officer.

Cas   0

APPENDIX 1
Men from Bilsdale who served in the Great War
Those who came back

John Arcoat Ainsley, son of William and Dorothy Ainsley (née Barr) of Spout House/Sun Inn. Born c.1898. Served with the Inniskilling Fusiliers.

Edgar Atkinson, son of William and Sarah Elizabeth Atkinson (née Helm) of High Crossletts, Raisdale. Born on 8th November 1893. Service number 89282, Gunner, 101 Company, Royal Garrison Artillery, Signaller, Manora India.

Stephen George Bennison, (known as 'Boy'), son of Joseph and Mary Ann Bennison (née Garbutt) of Broadfield. Born c.1887. Served with the Inniskilling Fusiliers. He was gassed and this affected his breathing for the rest of his life.

George Brotton, son of Robert Pickering and Anne Brotton (née Garbutt) of Ella Bridge. Baptised 11th March 1894. Served in Durban, South Africa.

Frank Burrell, husband of Sarah (née Leng). Originally from Ireland, he was a school teacher at Chop Gate

Frank Cook, son of Thomas and Mary Ann Cook (née Bell). Born c.1897. During the War his knee cap was blown off and he convalesced on the Isle of Arran.

Harry Cook, son of Thomas and Mary Ann Cook (née Bell), known as "Sloper". Born c.1887. He served with the Lancashire Fusiliers and lost a leg during the War.

Frederick Featherstone, son of Joseph and Elizabeth Featherstone, farmer of Stableholme. Baptised August 7th 1892. Served in Mesopotamia.

Robert Garbutt, son of George and Margaret Garbutt (née Hoggart) of Cockflat. Baptised 11th September 1887. He left home quite young and emigrated to Canada. It is uncertain whether he enlisted in Canada or England.

William Hoggart, son of George and Jane Hoggart (née Johnson) of Clay House, Chop Gate. Baptised 26th June 1892.

Thomas Hugill, son of Margaret Hugill of Malkin Bower (near Fangdale Beck). Born c.1891.

Alfred Thomas Johnson, son of Isaac and Jane Johnson. Born c.1894. Was a Corporal in the Green Howards.

John Henry (Jack) Johnson, son of John and Hannah Johnson (née Atkinson) of Fangdale Beck. Born c.1897. Served in the Medical Corps.

Lancelot Francis Johnson, son of Garbutt and Jane Johnson of the Buck Inn, Chop Gate. Baptised 13th October 1889.

Thomas W Johnson, son of John and Hannah Johnson (née Atkinson) of Fangdale Beck. Born c.1882. John and Thomas were both joiners. He enlisted in 1914 and served in the Royal Artillery, but was in Britain for the duration of the war.

Clarence Leng, son of John Thomas and Elizabeth Leng (née Garbutt), who lived at Westcote, before moving to Busby. Baptised 10th May 1896. He served with the Royal Artillery and of the 222 men in his unit, only 13 returned.

William Metcalfe, son of William and Hannah Metcalfe (née Wilson). Baptised 22nd November 1896. He was a local preacher who lived in Raisdale.

Fred Noble, son of Annie Noble of Cowslip. Born c.1894.

Harold Noble, son of Richard and Elizabeth Ann Noble (née Atkinson) of The Grange. Baptised 19th September 1886. Served with the Royal Artillery in Salonika.

William Noble, thought to be the son of Annie Noble of Cowslip, brother of Fred. Born c.1886.

James Peacock, son of Isaac and Annie E Peacock of Forge Cottage, Chop Gate. Born c.1898. Served with the Royal Engineers in Dover.

Joseph Prest, son of George William and Ann E Prest of Wain End, Laskill Pasture. Did not return to Bilsdale.

William Prest, son of George William and Ann E Prest of Wain End, Laskill Pasture. Born c.1892.

Fred Ward, of Fangdale Beck. Served with the Royal Engineers.

Arthur Weatherall, son of Davison and Jane Weatherall of Spout House Cottage. Born c.1896.

Jack Weatherall (known as John), son of Davison and Jane Weatherall of Spout House Cottage. Baptised 7th August 1881.

William Medd Weatherall (known as Medd), son of Davison and Jane Weatherall of Spout House Cottage. Born c.1894. Served with the Royal Flying Corps.

Those who did not come back Commemorated in Fangdale Beck

Ernest Allison, died 14th February 1918, aged 24. Son of J. W. and Frances Ann Hart of Oxfield House, South Broughton/Cow Helm, Bilsdale. Private 41472, 2nd Battalion, Royal Inniskilling Fusiliers. Died in hospital in Belfast. Buried in St. John the Divine Churchyard, Fangdale Beck.

Harold Atkinson, died 9th August 1915, aged 19. Son of John and Elizabeth Atkinson, of Castle Hills, Worsall, originally from Crosset. Private 15147, 6th Battalion, East Yorkshire Regiment. Commemorated on the Helles Memorial, Gallipoli Peninsula, Turkey.

Charles William Reginald Duncombe, died 15th September 1916, aged 37. Son of William Reginald Duncombe, Viscount Helmsley, elder son of 1st Earl of Feversham. Lieutenant Colonel, Yorkshire Hussars Yeomanry; commanding 21st Battalion. King's Royal Rifle Corps. Buried in plot III. L. 29, A.I.F. Burial Ground, Flers, Somme, France.

John Thomas Garbutt, died 14th November 1916, age unknown. Nephew of Francis and Martha Wilson (née Garbutt) of Laskill Pasture. Rifleman S/4170, 13th Battalion, Rifle Brigade. Commemorated on the Thiépval Memorial, Somme, France.

John William Garbutt, died 7th June 1917, born c.1892. Son of William and Annie Garbutt (née Ainsley) of High Ewe Cote, Bilsdale. Private 32549, 8th Battalion, York and Lancaster Regiment. Buried in plot II. J. 18, Perth Cemetery (China Wall), near Ypres, Belgium.

Joseph Garbutt, died 16th June 1919, aged 36. Son of George and Annie Garbutt, of The Grange, Bilsdale. Sapper WR/273517, The Royal Engineers. Buried in St. John the Divine Churchyard at Fangdale Beck.

Commemorated in
St. Hilda's Church / Chop Gate Village

Harry Ainsley, died 29th August 1918, aged 27. Son of the late Stephen and Charity Ainsley, (née Featherstone) formerly of Ella Bridge, Bilsdale. Corporal TS/4592, 1061st Company, Army Service Corps. Died of Malaria in 80th General Hospital, Salonika. Buried in plot 50 Kirechkoi-Hortakoi Military Cemetery, near Thessaloniki, Greece.

Percy William Allenby, died 7th September 1916, aged 21. Grandson of William and Mary Allenby, husband of Elizabeth May Allenby, of 98 Lumley St, Middlesbrough. Private 4481, 4th Battalion, Yorkshire Regiment. Buried in Linthorpe Cemetery, Middlesbrough.

Robert Etherington, died 25th February 1919, aged 41. Son of Christopher and Selina Etherington, of Seamer. Private 18985, Yorkshire Regiment. Also served with Labour Corps and had been transferred to 654960, 352nd Prisoner of War Company. Buried in St. Cuthbert Churchyard, Kildale.

John William Garbutt (known as Jack), died 21st March 1918, aged 22. Son of Issac and Mary Emma Garbutt (née Hardwick), of Wingroves, Bilsdale. Bombardier 63978. C Battery, 94th Brigade, Royal Field Artillery. Commemorated on the Pozières Memorial, near Albert, France.

Harry Knaggs, died 14ᵗʰ November 1918, aged 25. Son of Levi and Jane Knaggs, (née Garbutt) of Halterley, Bilsdale. Private 72496, 2nd Battalion West Yorkshire Regiment (Prince of Wales's Own). Buried in plot B. 23, Douai British Cemetery, Cuincy, Northern France.

William Tasker, died 24ᵗʰ February 1919, aged 35. Son of John and Elizabeth Tasker. Driver T3/026629, Royal Army Service Corps. Buried in St. John the Baptist and all Saints Churchyard, Easingwold.

Henry Trousdale, died 2ⁿᵈ July 1917, born c.1885. Son of John and Alice Trousdale, of Beacon Guest and later Ellermire. Private 44019, 22ⁿᵈ Battalion, Durham Light Infantry. Buried in plot I. C. 9, Belgian Battery Corner Cemetery, Ypres, Belgium.

Clarence Elwyn Wilson, died 10ᵗʰ August 1915, aged 23. Son of Joseph Percy and Louisa Wilson, of Cam House, Chop Gate, Stokesley, Middlesbrough. Private 10904, 6ᵗʰ Battalion, Yorkshire Regiment. Commemorated on the Helles Memorial, Gallipoli Peninsula, Turkey.

Author's note: it is acknowledged that this list of Bilsdale men who served in the Great War may not be complete. Anyone with additional information is asked to make contact so that amendments can be made.

References

Frontispiece

1. *Poems of the Great War,* p17

Chapter 1

1. *Surnames of the UK,* p158
2. *Bygone Bilsdale,* p20
3. Feversham Archive
4. *Bygone Bilsdale,* p18
5. Information provided in notes written by Stanley Isaac Garbutt
6. St. Hilda's, Bilsdale baptism register
7. *The Local Records of Stockton and the Neighbourhood,* (page unknown)
8. Information from Ruth Rudd, March 2006

Chapter 2

1. *Bilsdale Surveys,* p2
2. *Bilsdale Surveys,* p35
3. *Bilsdale Surveys,* p91
4. *Bilsdale Surveys,* p129
5. Bilsdale Midcable Assessment
6. *Bilsdale Estate - Sale Catalogue*
7. *Bygone Bilsdale,* p31-2
8. Bilsdale Midcable, Chop Gate CE School Log Book 1890-1906

Chapter 3

1. Bilsdale Midcable, Chop Gate CE School Register
2. Bilsdale Midcable, Chop Gate CE School Log Book 1890-1906

3. All quotations in this section are from Bilsdale Midcable, Chop Gate CE School Log Book 1890-1906
4. All quotations from this point are from the Board of Education File on Chopgate School 1872-1918

Chapter 4

1. *The First World War,* p34
2. *Tommy,* p33
3. *Your Country Needs You,* p59
4. *Field Service Pocket book, 1914,* p179
5. *Tommy,* p163
6. *Mud, Blood and Poppycock,* p139
7. *Mud, Blood and Poppycock,* p144
8. *Mud, Blood and Poppycock,* p20
9. *Tommy,* p163
10. Adapted from www.1914-1918.net/
11. *Mud, Blood and Poppycock,* p140
12. www.1914-1918.net/
13. *Tommy,* p399
14. *Tommy,* p404
15. Information provided by Tom Tulloch-Marshall, August 2006
16. *Tommy,* p409
17. *Your Country Needs You,* p85
18. www.raf.mod.ukrafhalton/aboutus/history.cfm
19. Letters 1914 - 15, number 3
20. www.cwgc.org/cwgcinternet/about.html
21. Letters 1914 - 15, number 3
22. Letters 1914 - 15, number 4
23. Letters 1914 - 15, number 4
24. Letters 1914 - 15, number 8
25. Letters 1914 - 15, number 10
26. *Your Country Needs You,* p87

27. Quoted in *Major and Mrs Holt's Concise Illustrated Battlefields Guide - The Western Front (North)* p144
28. War Diary - 94th Brigade Royal Field Artillery
29. www.westernfrontassociation.com/thegreatwar/ articles/timeline/loos.html
30. *Your Country Needs You,* p88
31. www.firstworldwar.bham.ac.uk/nicknames/campbell. html
32. *Tommy,* p198
33. Letters 1916, number 2
34. War Diary - 21st Division Senior Supply Officer
35. War Diary - 96th Brigade Royal Field Artillery
36. War Diary - 96th Brigade Royal Field Artillery

Chapter 5

1. *The Price of Glory, Verdun 1916,* p327
2. War Diary - 96th Brigade Royal Field Artillery
3. Letters 1916, number 5
4. War Diary - CRA 21st Division September 1915 - December 1916
5. War Diary - CRA 21st Division September 1915 - December 1916
6. *Tommy,* p314
7. *Field Service Pocket book, 1914,* p168
8. War Diary - 21st Division Senior Supply Officer
9. War Diary - 21st Division Senior Supply Officer
10. War Diary - 33rd Mobile Veterinary Section
11. War Diary - CRA 21st Division September 1915 - December 1916
12. War Diary - 21st Division Senior Supply Officer
13. *The First Day on the Somme,* p105
14. *Storm of Steel,* p95
15. War Diary - CRA 21st Division September 1915 - December 1916

16. From the *Official History of the Great War,* quoted in *The First Day on the Somme,* p263
17. War Diary - CRA 21st Division September 1915 - December 1916
18. War Diary - 21st Division Senior Supply Officer
19. War Diary - 33rd Mobile Veterinary Section
20. War Diary - CRA 21st Division September 1915 - December 1916
21. War Diary - 94th Brigade Royal Field Artillery
22. Letters 1916, number 15
23. Letters 1916, number 16

Chapter 6

1. *The First World War,* p88
2. *The First World War,* p89
3. *The Kaiser's Battle,* p36
4. War Diary - CRA 21st Division January - June 1917
5. Letters 1917, number 3
6. Letters 1917, number 5
7. Letters 1917, number 7
8. Letters 1917, number 7
9. War Diary - 21st Division Senior Supply Officer
10. www.westernfrontassociation.com/thegreatwar/articles/timeline/arras.html
11. War Diary - 94th Brigade Royal Field Artillery
12. *Tommy,* p53
13. Letters 1917, number 9
14. *Field service pocket book, 1914,* p179
15. www.tochparticipation.co.uk/aboutus.htm
16. War Diary - CRA 21st Division July 1917-1919
17. www.westernfrontassociation.com/thegreatwar/articles/timeline/messines.html
18. *Tommy,* p56

19. From J H Boraston (Ed), *Sir Douglas Haig's Despatches,* London 1919, p106 quoted in *Tommy,* p57
20. *The War Poems,* p137
21. War Diary - CRA 21st Division July 1917-1919
22. War Diary - CRA 21st Division July 1917-1919
23. www.westernfrontassociation.com/thegreatwar/ articles/timeline/ypres3.html
24. War Diary - 33rd Mobile Veterinary Section
25. Letters 1917, number 16
26. War Diary - 94th Brigade Royal Field Artillery
27. Letters 1917, number 25
28. War Diary - 21st Division Senior Supply Officer
29. *The Kaiser's Battle,* p18

Chapter 7

1. *The First World War,* p120
2. *The First World War,* p116
3. *All Quiet on the Home Front,* p192/279
4. War Diary - 94th Brigade Royal Field Artillery
5. War Diary - 94th Brigade Royal Field Artillery
6. War Diary - 94th Brigade Royal Field Artillery
7. Letters 1918, number 1
8. Letters 1918, number 2
9. War Diary - 21st Division Senior Supply Officer
10. *The Kaiser's Battle,* p21
11. *The Kaiser's Battle,* p52
12. The War Diary - 94th Brigade Royal Field Artillery says 4.30 - 4.45am, but many other sources state the time at 4.40am
13. From *Steel Wind: Colonel Georg Bruchmuller and the Birth of Modern Artillery,* David T Zabecki (London 1994), p74 quoted in *Tommy,* p405
14. *The Kaiser's Battle,* p178

15. War Diary - 21st Division General Staff HQ Diary
16. *The Kaiser's Battle,* p308
17. *The Kaiser's Battle,* p322
18. *All Quiet on the Home Front,* p94-95

Chapter 8

1. *The Kaiser's Battle,* p348
2. *Tommy,* p274-5
3. www.westernfrontassociation.com/thegreatwar/articles/timeline/aisne3.html
4. War Diary - 94th Brigade Royal Field Artillery
5. War Diary - 94th Brigade Royal Field Artillery
6. *Tommy,* p625
7. *Tommy,* p89
8. *Tommy,* p274-5
9. www.visionofbritain.org.uk/census/index.jsp
10. www.1914-1918.net/
11. 1901 census
12. Research carried out in Bilsdale by Ida Atkinson, 2006
13. www.1914-1918.net/
14. www.1914-1918.net/
15. Research carried out in Bilsdale by Ida Atkinson, 2006
16. Information from Bilsdale War Memorials
17. *The Kaiser's Battle,* p320
18. Letter from Gladys Wilmore dated 5 March 1981
19. Letter from Gladys Wilmore dated 5 March 1981
20. Letter from Gladys Wilmore dated 15 May 1981
21. Letter from Gladys Wilmore dated 27 May 1982
22. www.cwgc.org/cwgcinternet/cemetery_details.aspx?cemetery=23104&mode=1
23. From *For the Fallen,* Laurence Binyon, 1914; taken from - *The Faber Book of War Poetry,* p575

Notes and Abbreviations

General Notes

1. All spellings and punctuation are as in the original document and have not been corrected.

2. All distances are given "as the crow flies"

War Diary Extracts

1. Abbreviations listed alphabetically

2/Lt	2nd Lieutenant
a/Bdr	Acting Bombardier
ADVS	Assistant Director of Veterinary Services
AFA	Army Field Artillery or Australian Field Artillery
Amm Col	Ammunition Column
AVC	Army Veterinary Corps
BA Col	Brigade Ammunition Column
Bdr	Bombardier
BSM	Battery Sergeant-Major
C/94	C Battery, 94th Brigade.
Capt	Captain
Cas	Casualty
CMG	Companion of the Order of St. Michael and St. George
Cpl	Corporal
CRA	Commander of the Royal Artillery
DA	Divisional Artillery
Dr	Driver
DSO	Distinguished Service Order
FOO	Forward Observation Officer
Ftr	Fitter

Gnr	Gunner
GOC (RA)	General Officer Commanding (Royal Artillery)
GSW	Gun Shot wounds
HE	High Explosive
Hons	Honours
How	Howitzer
LI	Light Infantry
Lt	Lieutenant
MG	Machine Gun
MO	Medical Officer
NCO	Non-Commissioned Officer
OC or O/C	Officer Commanding
OO	Operational Orders
OP	Observation Post / Point
OR	Other Ranks
Pdr	Pounder
Pnr	Pioneer
RE	Royal Engineers
RFA	Royal Field Artillery
RFC	Royal Flying Corps
RGA	Royal Garrison Artillery
Sgt	Sergeant
TM	Trench Mortar

2. The letters in brackets (A, B, C, D) after names show the battery of the man concerned.

3. In the heading for each month the following information is given if it appeared in the original:
   - Name of the person who wrote the diary for the month
   - Location of the brigade HQ at the start of the month
   - Map references

4. In the war diary sections various map references and details of operational orders are quoted as they appear in the original. For example:

    • Map references - C29c.4½.9½ or J5c.7.1 or M17d.93.14 or N24a.

    • Operational orders - 21st DA 00 No4 (21st Divisional Artillery, Operational Orders, Number 4).

    These and references to other orders, are shown in italics.

5. In the casualty lists at the end of each month for the 94th Brigade Diary, the numbers at the start of each line refer to the date the injury or death took place.

Bibliography – Sources quoted in the text

The author is grateful to the copyright holders of these sources for permission to quote from them.

Books

Ashcroft, M. Y. and Hill A. M. eds. 1980. *Bilsdale Surveys 1637-1851,* North Yorkshire County Council Record Office.

Baker, K. 1997 *The Faber Book of War Poetry.* Faber and Faber.

Bilsdale Study Group. 1992. *Bygone Bilsdale.*

Corrigan, G. 2003. *Mud, Blood and Poppycock,* Cassell Plc, a division of The Orion Publishing Group (London).

General Staff, War Office. *Field Service Pocket Book 1914,* Reprinted by The Naval and Military Press Ltd.

Harrison, H. 1912-18. *Surnames of the UK, Volume 1,;* Eaton press.

Holmes, R. 2004. *Tommy,* Harper Collins Publishers Ltd. Copyright © 2004 Richard Holmes.

Holt, T & V. 2004. *Major and Mrs Holt's Concise Illustrated Battlefields Guide - The Western Front (North),* Pen and Sword Books.

Horne, A. 1964. *The Price of Glory,* Verdun 1916, Penguin Books, Pan Macmillan, London. Copyright © Alistair Horne, 1964.

Howard, M. 2002. *The First World War,* OUP. By permission of Oxford University Press.

Jünger, E. 2003. *Storm of Steel,* translated by Michael Hoffman; (Allen Lane, The Penguin Press, 2003.) Copyright © Michael Hofmann, 2003.

Middlebrook, M. 1971/2001 *The First Day on the Somme,* Penguin Books.

Middlebrook, M. 1978. *The Kaiser's Battle,* Book Club Associates/ Allen Lane.

Middlebrook, M. 2000. *Your Country Needs You,* Pen and Sword Books.

Richmond, T. *The Local Records of Stockton and the Neighbourhood,* By permission of The Durham County Record Office, Reference B113.

Penguin Books. 1998. *Poems of the Great War,* Penguin.

Sassoon, G. 1983. S Sassoon *The War Poems,* Faber and Faber. Copyright © Siegfried Sassoon by kind permission of the Estate of George Sassoon.

Van Emden, R. and Humphries, S. 2003. *All Quiet on the Home Front,* Headline Book Publishing.

Wrigley, A. & Sons. 1944. *Bilsdale Estate - Sale Catalogue,* The Waverley Press.

Public records

St. Hilda's Bilsdale Parish Baptism Register; North Yorkshire County Council Record Office - Film MIC 775.

Feversham Archive ZEW IV; North Yorkshire County Council Record Office - Film 1566.

Bilsdale Midcable Assessment; The National Archives - IR 58/58584.

Bilsdale Midcable, Chop Gate CE School Log Book 1890-1906; North Yorkshire County Council Record Office - Film 3736.

Bilsdale Midcable, Chop Gate CE School Register; North Yorkshire County Council Record Office - Film 3116.

Board of Education File on Chopgate School 1872-1918; The National Archives - ED 21/19352.

War Diary - 94th Brigade Royal Field Artillery; The National Archives - WO 95/2141.

War Diary - 96th Brigade Royal Field Artillery; The National Archives - WO 95/2143.

War Diary - 97th Brigade Royal Field Artillery; The National Archives - WO 95/2143.

War Diary - CRA 21st Division September 1915 - December 1916; The National Archives - WO 95/2136.

War Diary - CRA 21st Division January - June 1917; The National Archives - WO 95/2137.

War Diary - CRA 21st Division July 1917-1919; The National Archives - WO 95/2138.

War Diary - 21st Division General Staff HQ; The National Archives - WO 95/2133.

War Diary - 21st Division Senior Supply Officer, 21 Divisional Train ASC, September 1915 - December 1916; The National Archives - WO 95/2149.

War Diary - 33rd Mobile Veterinary Section, September 1915 - March 1919; The National Archives - WO 95/2148.

1901 Census for Bilsdale; The National Archives - RG 13/4550 and 4592.

Websites - all accessed on 6th January 2008

Statistics and Divisional Histories: The Long, Long Trail, Chris Baker - www.1914-1918.net/

Descriptions of events in major battles
www.westernfrontassociation.com/thegreatwar/articles/timeline/

The Commonwealth War Graves Commission
www.cwgc.org/

General information
www.firstworldwar.bham.ac.uk/

The History of RAF Halton
www.raf.mod.uk/rafhalton/aboutus/history.cfm

Toc H
www.tochparticipation.co.uk/aboutus.htm

National Census Information
www.visionofbritain.org.uk/census/index.jsp

Sources used for background research but not quoted in the text

Books

Chapman, P. 2000. *A Haven in Hell* (Talbot House, Poperinghe), Pen and Sword Books.

Coombs, R.E.B. 1994. *Before Endeavours Fade,* After the Battle Publications.

Articles

Butcher, B *Vets in War;* in Stand To (The Journal of the Western Front Association) № 71.

Clarke, B. *The Story of the British War Horse from Prairie to Battlefield,* from The Great War Magazine, Part 159.

Websites

The Menin Gate.
www.fylde.demon.co.uk/menin.html

Photographs

The author would like to thank the following for permission to reproduce photographs: The Imperial War Museum for photographs on pages 54, 55, 92, 95, 143 and 146, and Ida Atkinson for photographs on pages 29, 32 and 48.

All other photographs reproduced belong to members of the family - thanks to everyone who allowed us to borrow these.

About the Author.

Susan Laffey, née Garbutt was born and brought up in County Durham where she became a lifelong supporter of Sunderland AFC. According to her degree certificate, she studied French at the University of Leicester, but the most rewarding part of her course by far was a final year dissertation, completed with the help of the Economic and Social History department, about the effects of the First World War in France.

She became a teacher in 1988 and is now Deputy Headteacher of a large secondary school in Staffordshire. She lives in Kidderminster with her husband, a pond full of goldfish and, occasionally, a visiting hedgehog. She can be contacted at: bilsdalebombardier@blueyonder.co.uk.